Victorian Comics

The Funny Wonder 191; 26 September 1896 (Tom Browne)

"HEADS OF THE PEOPLE."
No. 1.—A. SLOPER, Esq., M.P., F.O.M., T.O.E., T.W.M., P.B., etc., etc.
THE UNIVERSAL WATCH PROVIDER.

Ally Sloper's Half-Holiday 130; 23 October 1886 (W. G. Baxter)

Victorian Comics

Denis Gifford

FAMOUS COMIC POSTERS.—No. 6.

GOD·SAVE·THE·QUEEN

Comic Cuts ½d

WHAT would the nation do without its Queen? Worse: What would the Queen do without her COMIC CUTS?

London GEORGE ALLEN & UNWIN LTD

RUSKIN HOUSE · MUSEUM STREET

Big Budget 154; 26 May 1900 (Ralph Hodgson)

ACKNOWLEDGEMENTS

All the illustrations in this book, save for a few photocopies, come from the collection of the author. Acknowledgement is made to the I.P.C. Publications (Juveniles Division) who hold the copyright in many of the Alfred Harmsworth comics.

For the sake of authenticity throughout this book the comics have been reproduced without any touching up or other doctoring. The reader will find that in some instances the captions are faded, since the comics are between seventy-five and a hundred years old.

For Pandy

(No connection with the Pandora Publishing Co.)

First Published 1976

ISBN 0 04 741002 7

Filmset and printed Offset Litho in Great Britain by Cox & Wyman Ltd, London, Fakenham and Reading

CONTENTS

The Comic Paper   page 6
The Comic Hero   27
The Comic Kid   55
The Comic Animal   66
The Comic Age   78
The Comic World   106
The Comic War   120
The Comic Artist: *index*   141

Ally Sloper's Half-Holiday 317; 24 May 1890 (Archibald Chasemore)

Vol. 1.   To be Published every Monday (for Saturday) at the Office, Red Lion House, Fleet Street, London.   No.

A WEEKLY BUDGET OF

FUNNY PICTURES—FUNNY NOTES   FUNNY JOKES—FUNNY STORIES.

SATURDAY, DECEMBER 12, 1874.]   "Our True Intent is all for your Delight."—SHAKESPEARE.   [PRICE ONE PENNY

The Comic Paper

MR COMIC CUTS AT COURT

The Uncrowned King of Comic Journalism presenting a copy of his Saturday Edition to the Queen of Great Britain and Empress of India—God bless her! (Ratts! This is orl tommy rott, gentile reeder. The old 'un's only bin at Court wunce, and then he cum home forty shillins short.—B. Winkle, Orfis-boy to the *Funny Wonder*!)

The original caption to the cartoon on the front of *The Funny Wonder* No. 191 dated 26 September 1896—the cartoon which appears on page 1 of this collection —sums up the story of the Victorian comic paper. British enterprise, British business, British patriotism, British humour. It also celebrates British style, for it was drawn by Tom Browne, the cartoonist who created British comic technique. Originally invented to bring low-cost laughter to the less than literate, plus profits to their publishers, comic papers continue in like vein to this very day: one of the more enduring institutions of the Victorian Age. The rough and the tumble, the bash and the splash, the black-eye and the bandage, are as basic to today's *Beano* as to yesterday's *Chips*. The cop and the robber, the kid and the teacher, and tucked away in corners, the dog and the mog, still fight the good and funny fight eighty years on and bid fair to make their century. Comics are a continuing saga, and there lies the rub: there is no point in their history where we can pick up a particular paper and proclaim it Comic Number One. This makes comics intriguing to the historian, infuriating to the collector. But begin they did, and their roots are squarely within that era of yesterday labelled Victorian.

Queen Victoria succeeded William IV on 20 June 1837; four years later *Punch* was born (17 July 1841). It was the latest and, as it turns out, the longest lived, in a long line of comic magazines inspired by the French *Figaro*. These weeklies were of a higher class than the illustrated broadsheets of the streets: more middle than working. The humour was satirical, the tone political, and there was none of the 'squinting eyes, wooden legs, and pimpled noses' which, according to William Makepeace Thackeray, 'form the chief points of fun' in the 'outrageous caricatures' of C. J. Grant, mainstay of such broadside series as *Every Body's Album* (1834). A marriage of the two classes came with the publication of an obvious *Punch* pinch, *Judy* (1 May 1867). The format followed the tradition for weekly magazines, a handy $8\frac{3}{4} \times 11\frac{1}{4}$ in., with one page given over to the topical

Ally Sloper's Half Holiday

BEING A SELECTION, SIDE-SPLITTING, SENTIMENTAL, AND SERIOUS, FOR THE BENEFIT OF OLD BOYS, YOUNG BOYS, ODD BOYS GENERALLY, AND EVEN GIRLS.

No. 1.]   SATURDAY, MAY 3, 1884.   [ONE PENNY.

cartoon, as such caricatured comment had been called since *Punch* published John Leech's 'Substance and Shadow' on 15 July 1843. It was not until *Judy* was three months old that something remarkable occurred within her pages.

It was called 'Some of the Mysteries of Loan and Discount' and it was a full page story told in pictures (p. 26). It was contributed by a prolific parodist and penny dreadful purveyor whose rough sketches were finished in ink for him by his seventeen-year-old French wife. Within two years Charles Henry Ross was the Editor of *Judy*, Mrs Ross ('Marie Duval', née Isabelle Émilie de Tessier) his leading cartoonist, and their character Ally Sloper a national institution. Ally, with his weekly adventures in pictures, qualifies as the first true British comic strip hero. He was the first to appear in comicbook format (*Ally Sloper: A Moral Lesson*, a paperback reprint collection of 216 pages and 750 pictures was published in November 1873, price one shilling), the first to have his own comic paper (*Ally Sloper's Half-Holiday* published weekly from 3 May 1884), and the longest lived in comic history (the last regular *Half-Holiday* was on 29 September 1923, the very last published in Scotland in 1949).

The magazine format was not to prove the ideal one for the comic paper. It was James Henderson who unfolded the average sixteen pages into an eight-page tabloid, $11 \times 16\frac{1}{2}$ in., and called his fifty-fifty combination of text and cartoons *Funny Folks*, 'A Weekly Budget of Funny Pictures, Funny Notes, Funny Jokes, Funny Stories'. One penny every Monday, No. 1 was published on 12 December 1874, and carried an editorial introduction in verse.

> Funny Folks! 'Tis just a budget,
> Full of pictures, jokes and fun,
> Pleasantly and not unkindly
> Showing what is said and done.
> Funny Folks, it seems to tickle,
> Funny Folks presents to view
> As a camera that all things
> To its Funny focus drew.

On the front was a large topical cartoon by John Proctor, and inside a 'Comic Fancy Page' by Montbard, together with three strip cartoons, two of them foreign. The text pages included a detective story parody, 'The Horrible Disclosures of S. Probe', and a humorous column by 'Mrs Grundy'. Thus in shape, size, and style, *Funny Folks* founded the form that the British comic would cling to for three-quarters of a century. The basic difference was, of course, that like all its immediate ilk, *Funny Folks* was a picture paper for the adult, not the child.

7

NO. 1.—GRATIS COPY.

No. 2 will be published, THURSDAY, MARCH 12th, 1885, at 2 o'clock. No more Free Cop

OFFICES: 153 FLEET STREET, LONDON, E.C.

JACK and JILL

An Illustrated Weekly Journal for Boys and Girls.

No. 1.] SATURDAY, March 7, 1885. [One Penny

James Henderson was the first of the new breed of working man's publisher. He specialised in providing low-priced fun, fact and fiction, with no aspirations towards the rarer air of the monthly magazines, yet a cut above the broadsides of Seven Dials and the penny dreadfuls of Edward Lloyd. Henderson had entered publishing in Manchester with *The Weekly Budget* (1861), and then set up in London at Red Lion House, Red Lion Court, as a specialist in juvenile literature: *Our Young Folks' Weekly Budget* ran, with several variations in title, from 2 January 1871 to 31 October 1896. Henderson's biggest rival in popular publishing was George Newnes, who pioneered scrap-book journalism with his phenomenally successful *Tit-Bits* (22 October 1881). Immediately imitators abounded (*Rare Bits, Funny Bits, Pick'd Bits*), Henderson included. But where Newnes pasted up paragraphs of text, Henderson clipped pictures: *Scraps*, subtitled 'Literary and Pictorial, Curious and Amusing' (29 August 1883), was a collage of cartoons and comic strips cut from *Harper's Weekly* and *The Judge* (New York), *Fliegende Blätter* (Munich) and *La Caricature* (Paris). Henderson also avoided the *Tit-Bits* image by making *Scraps* match *Funny Folks* in size and shape. The popularity of these Henderson twins inspired the Brothers Dalziel to produce their 'Selection, Side-splitting, Sentimental, and Serious, for the Benefit of Old Boys, Young Boys, Odd Boys generally, and even Girls'. They called it *Ally Sloper's Half-Holiday.*

Gilbert Dalziel had taken over *Judy* in 1872. The great engraver had promptly raised the old girl's sights, aiming at the *Punch* market, but was careful not to interfere with the career of her star performer. The paperback reprints had become annual best-sellers with *Ally Sloper's Comic Kalendar* (1876–84), supplemented by *Ally Sloper's Summer Number* (1880–4) and such special editions as *Ally Sloper's Guide to the Paris Exhibition* (1878) and *Ally Sloper's Book of Beauty* (1880). Ally's own paper was the logical consequence. It is said that from it Dalziel made £30,000; what Ross made, if anything, is unrecorded. The first issue had two small Ross-Duval cartoons; both of them were reprints. In fact, all the Sloper strips in the *Half-Holiday* were reprints, many going back twenty years. It was the Sloper cartoons that made the *Half-Holiday*, huge panels that filled most of the front page and exploded across the entire centre spread every Christmas (back end-paper). Cartoons that set Sloper in the thick of any and every event of the day, from christening his latest offspring in honour of the Queen's Jubilee (p. 78) to being dubbed Baron Sloper of Mildew Court (front end-paper). This 'new look' Sloper was created by W. G. Baxter, a brilliant cartoonist born in America, raised in Buxton, and trained on the Manchester weekly *Momus*. His caricatures of local notables and occasions raised his status to Joint Editor, but

JACK'S JOURNAL

An Illustrated Weekly Miscellany for Everybody.

In continuation of "**JACK and JILL.**"

| ol. IV.—No. 115.] | SATURDAY, May 14, 1887. | [One Penny. |

he still found time to freelance for Dalziel's *Judy*. When *Momus* closed in 1883, Dalziel brought Baxter to London, and his first front page cartoon graced the tenth number of *Ally Sloper's Half-Holiday*. Ally himself did not appear until three weeks later, when Baxter drew him in full grog-blossom bloom holding a 'Hyde Park Demonstration' beneath a banner which proclaimed for the first time his famous slogan, 'Ally Sloper, the Friend of Man'. This was quickly condensed to 'F.O.M.', and soon a whole string of impressive but suspicious initials followed (p. 2). A much envied set was 'F.O.S.', the Friend of Sloper award, which was pictorially presented on the back page every week from 19 November 1887. The first went to G. H. Chirgwin, the White-Eyed Kaffir; the 963rd to Charles Ross, Junior, who wrote a weekly piece under the pseudonym of 'Tootsie Sloper'. Dalziel's other contribution to the comic was order. Instead of the jumble that was *Scraps*, Sloper readers could be sure of finding their favourite features in fixed spots in the paper. Text, spotted by small cartoons, was relegated to the alternate spreads of pages 2–3 and 6–7, making a refreshing break from the massed cartoons that filled the front, back, and middle. James Brown's slapstick Scots saga of 'The McNab', another hold-over from *Judy*, ran as a strip across the bottom of page 4; above these caber capers was 'Distinguished People Interviewed by A. Sloper' (anyone from J. L. Toole to Swinburne to the Prince of Wales was fair game for fun); opposite was the topical comment cartoon, 'Our Weekly Whirligig'. Dalziel's well-laid centre spread would become a characteristic feature of the British comic.

'The Largest Penny Illustrated Paper in the World' was the claim Davis and Marshall made for their *Illustrated Tid-Bits*, a sixteen paged penn'orth which began on 4 October 1884, and began again on 17 January 1885 as *Illustrated Bits* after George Newnes brought a law suit. There were other dramas during this comic's career, including changes of Publisher, Editor, policy, and size; but it also introduced the first deliberate attempt to discover strip cartoonists. Editor 'Bimbo' ran a Grand Prize Comic Tableaux Competition offering one pound for 'six small comic tableaux illustrating a story'. And so, besides creating a new field for artists, Bimbo coined the earliest known term for the comic strip—and acquired a supply of them at less than going rates!

The first comic specifically designed for children was *Jack and Jill*, published by W. Long on 7 March 1885. A charming scrapbook of sketches and verse, it had Edward Lear on the back page and was a total failure. With the eighth issue the subtitle was changed from 'An Illustrated Weekly Journal for Boys and Girls' to 'An Illustrated Journal for Everybody', and from 14 May 1887, the title itself was changed to *Jack's Journal*. It was now clear to publishers and purchasers that there existed two distinct classes of humorous journalism, the *Punch* school—both

SNACKS

A JOURNAL OF HUMOUR, ROMANCE, COMIC CUTS, AND ANSWERS ON EVERYTHING.

| VOL. I. No. 3. | SATURDAY, JULY 20, 1889. | [ONE PENN |

Pick-Me-Up (1888) and *The Jester* (1889) were in this magazine tradition, although their aim was comedy not comment—and the *Funny Folks* format—*Snacks* (15 June 1889) was clearly a comic. The most significant thing about this mainly reprint paper was its sub-head: 'A Journal of Humour, Romance, Comic Cuts, and Answers on Everything.' But before explaining this significance, to keep in strict chronology mention must be made of *Laughter*, 'A Weekly Budget of Mirth, Wit and Humour' published as a short-lived, sixteen-paged, half-size comic from 15 February 1890.

James Henderson employed a great many freelance contributors to help fill the columns of tiny type between the line-blocks. One of these hacks was a fifteen-year-old Irish lad called Alfred Charles William Harmsworth. This son of a barrister had so rapid and adept a turn of the pen that within two years he was made Assistant Editor of a boy's paper called *Youth* (1882). In 1885 Harmsworth went to Coventry to work on papers published by Iliffe & Sons, returning later to London to serve in the office of George Newnes. The continuing success of *Tit-Bits* and the comparative ease of its weekly compilation was inspiration to his ambition, and one month before his twenty-third birthday, Harmsworth, helped by his brothers, issued his own magazine from a small room on the first floor of 26 Paternoster Row. He called it *Answers to Correspondents*, and the print run for his No. 1, dated 12 June 1888, was 13,000. Within a year the circulation had almost quadrupled. Eager to enlarge, Harmsworth cast around for another success to simulate. He found it in *Funny Folks* and *Scraps*, published by his first employer, James Henderson. And so on 17 May 1890, from a slightly more salubrious address in Fleet Street (No. 145), Harmsworth issued the first edition of his second venture.

Comic Cuts was clearly not the first British comic, as its publishers would constantly claim throughout the fifty-three years of its life. Indeed, it looked like any of the many comics then on the market, and not only in size and format: it reprinted cartoons and strips that Henderson himself had reprinted five or more years before! Even its title was unoriginal: *Comic Cuts* had appeared in the sub-heading of *Snacks* the previous year, and anyway was standard trade jargon for a humorous engraving on a printing block: a 'cut' that was comic! But the new paper had the Harmsworth touch, the same touch that had made *Answers* a real rival to *Tit-Bits*: he sold it at half the regular price: 'One Hundred Laughs for One Halfpenny!' Wrote Harmsworth in his first editorial:

Remember the following facts about *Comic Cuts*. It is as large as any penny paper of the kind published; this you can prove by measurement. It employs the best artists, is printed on good paper, is published every Thursday, will give big prizes, is the first halfpenny illustrated ever issued, and has plenty of money behind it. How is it possible for anyone to provide an illustrated paper, containing nearly fifty pictures, over eighteen thousand words, and many valuable prizes, for a halfpenny? Well, it is possible to do it, but that is all.

Cheap reprints helped, of course; even the text was lifted from back numbers of *Answers*! But a small notice in No. 3 promised some hope for the future.

WANTED!

ORIGINAL SKETCHES

FOR

"COMIC CUTS."

HANDSOME PAY OFFERED.

PROFESSIONAL ARTISTS ONLY NEED APPLY.

The first Professional Artist was Roland Hill, and his first strip made the front page of No. 4. *Those Cheap Excursions* (p. 18) is typical of Hill's strips depicting the suburban scene. Next came Oliver Veal, who worked in the then-fashionable silhouette style (p. 19). Solids soon proved unsuitable for the cheaply printed comics, and Veal evolved a freer form that found him a full-time career as a strip cartoonist.

If Harmsworth's ha'porth had not actually started the comic in Britain, it had certainly started the comic boom. Number 1 sold out; wrote Harmsworth, 'I was at Nottingham the first day *Comic Cuts* appeared, and on asking for the paper was unable to get one in the whole town'. Number 2 sold out, too, and by the time Harmsworth sat down to compose his 'What the Editor Says' for No. 3, other publishers were busily preparing cut-price comics. 'Well, gentlemen,' wrote Harmsworth, 'I have got a good start, and you will have to put in several thousands of pounds, much hard work, and a few other attributes of success before you get ahead of the first halfpenny illustrated.' Secretly Harmsworth got busy on another comic of his own.

Funny Cuts hit the newsagents' shops on 2 July 1890, published by Trapps, Holmes & Co, neighbours and rivals of James Henderson in Red Lion Court. This eight page ha'penny was edited by Gordon Phillip Hood, whom Trapps and

ILLUSTRATED CHIPS

½d ½d

No. 1.—Vol. I. [ENTERED AT STATIONERS' HALL]   PRICE ONE HALFPENNY.   [TRANSMISSION ABROAD AT BOOK RATES.]   JULY 26, 189

Holmes introduced thus: 'We promise our readers that our Editor is the funniest man on earth. He is a very Samson or Sandow of humour. He is irresistible'. He was also pretty smart with the scissors, pasting up his pages with cartoons clipped from those American magazines which Harmsworth and Henderson had unaccountably missed. But by No. 16 (25 October) finances had improved sufficiently for Hood to give over his entire front page to Alfred Gray, an old hand from *Judy* and *Sloper* (pp. 42-3). *Funny Cuts* was a great success and ran for thirty years, clocking up 1,566 issues. Harmsworth's answer, his companion to *Cuts*, was a horrible failure and folded after six weeks. Or, rather, unfolded. . . .

Here you are, then! Here is the Editor with his bottle of hair-restorer by his side (N.B. He is a strict teetotaler so you needn't make any nasty insinuations), and his false teeth hung carefully on the gas bracket. Observe the kind and amiable expression on his face; look at the bags of gold in the corner.

Hardly Harmsworth, except perhaps for the bags of gold! He had called his new paper *Illustrated Chips*, taking the title from *Choice Chips*, a cheap imitator of *Tit-Bits*, vintage 1884. For once the famous Harmsworth touch failed him. He had halved his tabloid *Comic Cuts* to produce a smaller paper of more pages, sixteen for a halfpenny. It seemed a good idea, but the format of *Punch*-style weeklies was not popular with the working-class readers of comics. *Chips*, as it was colloquially called, was born on 26 July 1890, and quickly born again on 6 September. This No. 1 'New Series' was back in the tried and true format of *Comic Cuts*, an eight-page tabloid. On 6 June 1891, the paper turned pink, and stayed pink for fifty years. It was pink again when it died, hand in hand with its white paper partner, on 12 September 1953.

The Victorian comic age arrived with a rush. Henderson produced *Snap-Shots* on 9 August 1890, one month before *Chips* unfolded into tabloid. Henderson, unable to halve his price, doubled his page-count: *Snap-Shots* boasted sixteen picture-packed pages for one penny. It was a scrapbook, but an honest one. The sub-head read, 'Humorous Pictures and Amusing Reading chiefly from Advance Proofs of Current American Papers by Exclusive Arrangement'. By 1900 *Snap-Shots* reversed the *Chips* evolution by halving its page size, upping the count to twenty-four, and printing a Club Edition on art paper for twopence: it had become a magazine. Another reprint comic, this time back at a halfpenny, was *Skits*. Number one came from the British Publishing Company, yet another denizen of Red Lion Court, on 27 June 1891. *Skits* closed after twenty-three issues. Murray Ford did much better with *The Joker*, notching up a six-year run from 18 July 1891. The front page featured a single cartoon signed 'Frank C'.

No. 1.) NEW PAPER. NEW PAPER. NEW PAPER.

THE Comic Home Journal

FRIDAY EDITION OF 'CHIPS'

1½d

No. 1. [ENTERED AT STATIONERS' HALL.] PRICE ONE HALFPENNY. [TRANSMISSION ABROAD AT BOOK RATES.] MAY 11, 1895.

starring spotty, spectacled 'Tony Green' and his embarrassing escapades with his comely cousins, Lottie, Tottie and Dottie. *The Joker* was even racier than *Sloper*, and ran pin-up sketches of such stage sweeties as Miss Harriet Vernon in the series 'The Joker's Lady Friends'. Henderson tried a flier in the old broadside style: *The Comic Pictorial Sheet* was no more than an unwieldly one-page reprint, published twice weekly from 29 September 1891, in several different sizes. At the other end of the paper scale came his *Comic Pictorial Nuggets* (7 May 1892), a sixteen-page halfpenny half-tabloid that soon became *Nuggets* (26 November). This one was a reprint of reprints, proclaiming its source as 'From *Scraps*, *Snap-Shots*, *Young Folks*, and the publications of Red Lion House for Over Thirty Years'. Trapps, Holmes & Co. brought out their second title on 6 July 1892. *The World's Comic* (p. 107) was reputedly edited by Grandad Twiggle, but clearly the Samson or Sandow of Humour was at work again, and from No. 29 they admitted the Editor to be Gordon Phillip Hood. The comic ran for sixteen years before combining with its companion, *Funny Cuts*.

All this comical activity by no means daunted Harmsworth, and on 30 July 1892, appeared Alfred's first editorial for number one of *The Wonder*.

> Well, it is out at last. The new halfpenny paper you have heard so much about is in your hands. Don't you think it is a wonder? Did you ever see a paper like it before, one as big, with so many pictures, or with pictures so good, and all for a halfpenny? Why, it is positively giving you a twopenny paper for a quarter of its value!

Unfortunately Harmsworth's editorial effusions failed to wash with the reader: *The Wonder* was neither a novelty nor a bargain. It was large, matching the once-folded broadsheet of the daily newspaper, but at four pages it contained only marginally more than its twice-folded companion comics. Harmsworth's continual effort to produce something different was certainly creditable, but he was wasting his time. Just as his half-size *Chips* had failed to catch on, so did his double-size *Wonder*, and after a run of twenty-seven weeks he was forced to revert to his winning format of *Comic Cuts*. With a slight retitling to emphasise the comical content, *The Funny Wonder* began again on 4 February 1893. It was an immediate success and ran, with slight changes of title and format, to that familiar, final date of 12 September 1953.

George Emmett, a boys' paper publisher, entered the field on 8 August 1892, but left again after a mere six weeks: *Jolly Bits* ('from Jolly Books') lacked the comic touch. Much more fun was *Larks!* (1 May 1893), 'founded and conducted' by Gilbert Dalziel (p. 57). He issued it from 'The Sloperies' (99 Shoe Lane, E.C.)

HA'PORTH OF FUN!   ROARS OF LAUGHTER

you reading
N YEARS'
PENAL
RVITUDE,"
by
e Who Has
Done It?
This Page.

No. 10. Vol. 1.

½d 1 ONLY 2D THE Wonder.

Publishe
Every Satur
and on s
all the we
until t
followi
SATURDA

OCT. 1, 18

with the advice that 'a penn'orth of Sloper and a ha'porth of *Larks* every week ought to make the British Nation happy!' It did, for nine years. The power of the comic was felt in the land: Charles P. Sisley's 'Artistic Weekly' *Up-To-Date* suddenly switched to the new funny format on 12 August 1893, after a near-fatal flirtation with illustrated news. *The Champion Comic* appeared on 9 January 1894, as a companion to *The Joker*, but had to be incorporated with its more successful partner exactly two years later, in spite of the offer of '10s a week paid to you if laid up by an accident'. Henderson brought out *Varieties* as a follow-up to *Nuggets* on 12 May 1894. At thirty-two pages for one penny it was a bargain bundle, but of reprints. Its magazine size was matched by Trapps, Holmes, who published *Side-Splitters* on 6 August 1894: sixteen pages for a halfpenny. Alfred Gray, their staff cartoonist, was made Editor, but the venture failed, and nine weeks later it was incorporated into *The World's Comic*.

Alfred Harmsworth had his failures, too. He tried out a story paper in the comic format, calling it *The Boy's Home Journal*. After five disastrous issues he switched text for sketches and began it again as *The Comic Home Journal* (11 May 1895). He played doubly safe by linking the 'new' paper with *Chips*, featuring portraits of the Editor, Cornelius Chips, and the office boy, Philpot Bottles, in the heading, and pretending that the renovated comic was really 'the Friday Edition of *Chips*'. The stunt worked, and the comic ran for nine years. Gimmicks were the order of the day, and when C. Arthur Pearson entered the comic market on 19 June 1897, his *Big Budget* (p. 82) went one better than Henderson's *Nuggets* and *Varieties*, which each contained a sixteen-page supplement of fiction. *Big Budget*'s catchline was 'Three Papers for a Penny!' First came an eight-page comic, then the eight-page *Comrades' Budget*, and lastly the eight-page *Story Budget*: twenty-four tabloid-size pages for one penny! It could not last, they said, and it did not: but only four pages and the sectionalisation had been lost by the end of the year. Under the excellent editorship of Arthur Brooke, *Big Budget* settled down to a twelve-year stretch.

The Joker lost his sauce and his 'r', becoming *Jokes* with effect from 20 January 1898 (p. 74); the change extended his life by but twenty-two weeks. Now George Newnes, Harmsworth's old rival, entered comics and produced *The Halfpenny Comic* on 22 January 1898 (p. 48). His experienced touch ensured success, and the paper ran for nine years. *Comic Bits*, from the Unity Publishing Co., did less well. The first issue came out on 19 February 1898; the last ten weeks later. Pearson's companion to his *Big Budget* met with little more success, despite the apparent advantage of being hooked to the top comedy personality of the period: *Dan Leno's Comic Journal* (26 February 1898) lasted ninety-three weeks (p. 87). *The Monster*

½d

THE CHAMPION COMIC

MES A CHAMPION 'KNOCK OUT'

½c FOR VALUE

No. 1.—Vol. I.   TUESDAY, JANUARY 9, 1894.   ONE HALFPENNY.

Comic (15 March 1898), a ha'penny pink'un put out by the Sketchy Bits Company, reached No. 14 before it closed. It fell victim to the new nomenclature: comic it was, 'a comic' it was not. It was a magazine.

In America the comic was a late but fast developer. Like the British originals, it evolved out of the weekly humour magazines, *Puck*, *Life* and *Judge*. Unlike the British originals, it was not sold. Joseph Pulitzer and James Gordon Bennett gave their comics away with their rival Sunday papers, the New York *World* and *Herald*, from 1894. Strips appeared among the jokes almost immediately, but regular characters did not develop until 1896, and did not 'take over' the comics until 1900. Where the American comics beat the British was in the use of colour. They were in full colour from the start, while colour did not come to the British comic until 12 September 1896. It was, as might be expected, an Alfred Harmsworth enterprise. The Special Autumn Edition of *Comic Cuts* was a history-making mess. 'Printing in colours in this country has hitherto been a failure', editorialised Harmsworth, and this twelve-paged, four-coloured, twice-the-price edition proved that the tradition of the British printer was holding true. However, Harmsworth had faith and persisted in his experiments. Coloured Christmas numbers followed, with occasional specials for the companion papers, *Chips* and *Wonder*, but it was left to his rivals, Trapps and Holmes, to publish the first regular comic in colour. They called it, of course, *The Coloured Comic* (p. 36). It first appeared on 21 May 1898, and 'Mr C. C.' wrote from 'The Editor's Colour Box': '*The Coloured Comic* has been a long thought-out project. It has necessitated the outlay of huge capital, so large indeed that I wonder where it all comes from. Sometimes I think it can be that the proprietors have been to the Klondyke and struck oil!' Only the front page was printed in full colour, and only for seventy-two weeks, although the comic itself ran to 1906. It managed to justify the continued use of its title by printing in blue instead of the standard black.

James Henderson produced his first proper comic on 2 July 1898, and it was another 'first': instead of four pages of pictures and four of stories, he put pictures on every page. *Pictorial Comic Life*, 'The Amusing Picture Paper for the People', became the last new title of the Victorian era. The Queen died on 22 January 1901; *Pictorial Comic Life* on 21 January 1928. Clearly, comics had come to stay.

EVERY MONDAY.

No. 1.

For Week Ending
July 2, 1898.

½D PICTORIAL Comic-Life.

The Amusing Picture-Paper for The People.

8 Pages of Pictures.

½d.

Printed and Published by James Henderson, at Red Lion House, Red Lion-court, Fleet-street, London.

IN CANNIBAL-LAND.—AN EXPLORER'S CLEVER DOG.

"My master has a biscuit in his pocket. Wish I had it," thought the dog.

"Oh, lor'! no more biscuits! Here's an end of me!"

"Might as well die game."

"Never seen a dog stand on his tail, evidently."

"How does a somersault strike you, old boy?"

"Dear me! I never thought I'd live to see that biscuit."

[This Series will be continued next week.

THE ANNUAL BEANO.
Come what may, 'Arry must take his annual "beano." (Note—'Arriet strictly prohibited. this journey.)

Pictorial Comic-Life 1; 1 July 1898

"THE ROMANY ROSE," a splendid new Serial Story, commences in our Grand Easter No. next week. Usual price ½d.

ILLUSTRATED CHIPS

No. 396. VOL. XVI. (NEW SERIES.) [ENTERED AT STATIONERS' HALL] PRICE ONE HALFPENNY. [TRANSMISSION ABROAD AT BOOK RATES] APRIL 2, 1898.

WEARY WILLY AND TIRED TIM HAVE A LIVELY TIME AT TUDOR STREET.

1. "The other day two mysterious gentlemen called at Chips offices. 'Please, sir,' said the tall, slender baronet, 'can you tell us where we can find Mr. Chips? We have called for the purpose of breaking him in half.' 'Yes,' said Bottles; 'you'll find him at "Answers" office.'

2. "Then William and Timothy (for that is what they said their names were) walked across. 'Now for it!' Timothy was heard to remark — "now to scatter the double-dyed villain's giblets.'

3. "But as soon as the Editors saw them, they armed themselves, and prepared to assault the visitors. 'Great billiards!' cried the gents, 'we have tumbled into Sweeney Todd's by mistake!'

4. "But they had another try, for they meant to carry out their breaking intentions, and so knocked at the 'Funny Wonder' office. 'Be ready to squash him," murmured William. 'I'm yer squasher!' responded Tim.

5. "But the squashing (whatever that may be) was not done, for a ferocious animal sprang out of the office, and William and Timothy were once more put to flight, Timothy crying 'Murder!' loudly and William calling for his mother.

6. "Presently, however, they came to the poet's room. 'Ah!' smiled the short, stout nobleman, 'we shall find sympathy here, at least; and perhaps we shall come across Mr. Chips.' 'Per-haps!' said William; 'p'raps not.'

7. "But it appears that, owing to his having smashed up all the furniture of his last office, the Fighting Editor's quarters had been changed, and he it was who answered the knock. 'Whotdoyerwant?' he said sternly. And the visitors seemed somewhat surprised.

8. "They were even a little bit more startled when the mighty man of muscle heaved them through the office window. 'Oh!' gasped Timothy, 'I think we're having a drop too much!'

9. "And when the unfortunate fellows reached the ground, their enemies gathered round and jeered them. 'Ow did yer like it, Willy?' grinned Bottles. Poor fellows! I felt quite sorry for them.—Yours sincerely, THE NEW SUB-EDITOR."

Illustrated Chips 396; 2 April 1898 (Tom Browne)

½d. Comic Cuts. ½d.

ONE HUNDRED LAUGHS FOR ONE HALFPENNY.

No. 4. Vol. I.] Registered.   ONE HALFPENNY WEEKLY.   [June 7, 1890.

THOSE CHEAP EXCURSIONS!

Jones and Brown resolve to take a holiday. "There's an excursion, and I'm going down to Margate to get a good blow," said Jones to Brown, as they left the office. "Take my advice—don't!" said Brown.

Jones starts—5 a.m.—without breakfast.

Going down—five hours of this for Jones, who doesn't smoke.

He just has time for "a good blow."

And then the return journey—all night on a "siding."

Brown sleeps till noon—

Dines early and well—

Takes a walk over Hampstead Heath in the afternoon—

His girl to the play in the evening.

(Tuesday morning.) Brown fresh and smiling! Jones limp and lank!

Comic Cuts 4; 7 June 1890 (Roland Hill)

The characteristics of the comic are so universal that it seems pointless to detail them. Yet they took longer to evolve than did the comic paper itself. *Funny Folks*, the first, never got around to establishing a regular character, despite the obvious appeal of Ally Sloper in his *Half-Holiday*. Baxter and Thomas never drew Sloper as a strip, despite Ally's seventeen-year career in picture story form in *Judy*. Tom Browne drew several strips a week for six years before he tried repeating characters: then Weary Willie and Tired Tim became part of British history.

PICTURES! JOKES! STORIES!

½D ILLUSTRATED CHIPS ·½D

No. 1 (New Series). [Entered at Stationers' Hall.] PRICE ONE HALFPENNY. [Transmission Abroad at Book Rates.] SEPT. 6, 1890.

"IN THE SPRING (ALSO IN THE SUMMER) A YOUNG MAN'S FANCY LIGHTLY TURNS TO THOUGHTS OF LOVE."

"We must fly to-morrow! My father's consent can never be obtained," she said.

"Farewell, dearest! To-morrow, at eight o'clock, in Gipsy Lane!" said Adolphus.

But the irate parent overhears the conversation, and determines to thwart the wicked design.

Having made every preparation for a hasty flight, Adolphus is there at the appointed time.

"Ha! she comes! I know her footsteps so well. My happiness is now complete!"

"My dearest!" he cried in the blindness of his joy.

But he quickly discovers he has made a mistake—

And returns a crestfallen man, and evidently the worse for his adventure.

Illustrated Chips 1; 6 September 1890 (Oliver Veal)

A BIG CRICKET MATCH as reported by the Sporting Correspondents.

Comic Cuts 10; 19 July 1890 (Roland Hill)

½d. ComicCuts. ½d.

ONE HUNDRED LAUGHS FOR ONE HALFPENNY.

No. 51. Vol. II.] Registered. ONE HALFPENNY WEEKLY. [MAY 2, 1891.

 CLEVER ARTISTS SHOULD SUBMIT WORK TO THE EDITOR OF "COMIC CUTS,"
Enclosing large stamped envelope for return, in case of rejection. (IMMEDIATE PAYMENT.)

THE EDITOR AND THE WOULD-BE COMIC FIEND.

(1) The Editor was sitting in his sanctum knocking off a few hundred jokes for COMIC CUTS, when a head was thrust round the door, exclaiming: "Sir, I have here a comic drawing suitable for—" "Begone!" replied the Editor impatiently. (2) Scarcely had the Editor resumed his pen when the head appeared through the window, saying: "Sir, I have here a comic drawing suitable for—" "Vanish!" replied the Editor sternly. (3) The Editor once more turned to his work, muttering angrily, when he was again assailed by the head, which this time appeared down the chimney crying: "Sir, I have here a comic drawing suitable for—" "Wretch, leave me!" answered the Editor savagely.

(4) Sure of having effectually rid himself of his unwelcome visitor, the Editor dashed off a score of jokes, when he was maddened to desperation at beholding the head through the sky-light, saying "Sir, I have here a comic drawing suitable for—" (5) It was more than the Editor could bear. Dragging the man down, he stabbed him to the heart with his paper-knife. But even while his life's blood ebbed away, he muttered: "Sir, I have here a comic drawing suitable for—" (6) And every night as the clock strikes twelve a shrouded skeleton appears to the Editor, saying in sepulchral tones: "Sir, I have here a comic drawing suitable for—"

Comic Cuts 51; 2 May 1891 ('F.L.')

MR. COMIC CUTS AND THE WOULD-BE COMIC FIEND.

1. The Editor was sitting in his sanctum, knocking off a few hundred jokes for COMIC CUTS, when a head was thrust round the door, exclaiming: "Sir, I have here a comic drawing, suitable for—"
"Begone!" cried Mr. C. C. impatiently.

2. Scarcely had the Editor resumed his pen, when a head appeared through the window, saying: "Sir, I have here a comic drawing, suitable for—"
"Vanish!" replied the Editor sternly.

3. Mr. C. C. once more turned to his work muttering angrily, when he was again assailed by the head, which this time appeared down the chimney, crying: "Sir, I have here a comic drawing, suitable for—"
"Wretch, leave me!" answered the Editor savagely.

4. Sure of having effectually rid himself of his unwelcome visitor, Mr. C. C. dashed off a score of jokes, when suddenly he was maddened to desperation at beholding a head through the skylight, saying: "Sir, I have here a comic drawing, suitable for—"

5. It was more than Mr. C. C. could bear. Dragging the fiend down, he stabbed him to the heart with his paper-knife. But even while his life's blood ebbed away, he muttered: "Sir, I have here a comic drawing, suitable for—"

6. And every night as the clock strikes twelve, a shrouded skeleton appears to Mr. C. C., saying in sepulchral tones: "Sir, I have here a comic drawing, suitable for—"

Comic Cuts 441; 22 October 1898 (Roland Hill)

WARNING!

If the editors of other papers continue to copy COMIC CUTS *jokes, cases like the following will be numerous.*

He saw it in COMIC CUTS and he nearly laughed the head off his head.

Then he found it in *Prig'd Bits*. It was so good that he laughed again, though not so violently.

He was thunderstruck when he found that the editor of *The Joke Stealer* had cribbed it. "It's a little too much," he muttered; "I'm tired of that infernal joke."

A week later he was fairly staggered, for he found that *Snips* had slightly altered it, and labelled it original.

Finally, he took up a local paper, and that joke; but before he could read it reason gave way, and they led him off to the lunatic asylum, and chained him down in the padded room.

Comic Cuts 10; 19 July 1890

Big Budget 150; 28 April 1900 (Ralph Hodgson)

Pictures might be of any size or shape, or be arranged in 'artistic' designs (p. 22); neatly ruled frames did not become common until 1898, and then were generally confined to front pages. Stories were narrated in 'librettos', squibs of text that ran underneath each panel. When a rare attempt was made to tell a story in pictures alone (p. 23), it was supplemented by explanatory paragraphs on an inside page.

GIFT COUPON.
JOKER. No. 277.

1D.

The Joker

No. 277.—Old Series.
No. 40.—New Series.

Thursday, October 22, 1896.

ONE PENNY.

THE ADVENTURES OF MR. SIMPLE.
CHAPTER III.

For the Awful History, see page 627.

The Joker 277; 22 October 1896

ANOTHER COP.

The Halfpenny Comic 74; 17 June 1899 (Ernest Wilkinson)

The balloon was a device as yet unborn. Ernest Wilkinson created a brief vogue for explanatory placards (p. 24), while 'Yorick' (Ralph Hodgson) was the first to flirt with actual speech within the frame (p. 25). Yorick, forced to follow Tom Browne's line when that artist abandoned comics, helped to consolidate the style that by 1900 was becoming the standard: clean, neat, open linework spotted with well-balanced blacks, plus plenty of action. Action, simple slapstick in pictures: this was the completely new thing comics had to offer, the thing which the humorous magazines lacked. To understand a *Punch* cartoon you had to read a caption as long as a short story. Although it helped to read the captions in a comic, you could pick up the gist of the joke with no more effort than the flick of an eyeball. No wonder children liked comics, and no wonder, once that section of the reading public became financially viable, the children took them over.

Big Budget 160; 7 July 1900 (Ralph Hodgson)

1. "Hech! but the MacHaggis has found a bonnie lot of fowls," murmured the MacWeedrap, as he espied his old enemy strolling home through the night. "I suspect the laird will find his fowl-hoose empty in the morning."

2. But he changed his tone next morning when he found that, with the exception of the old rooster, all his own birds were missing. "Eh, mon, this is MacHaggis's work!" he groaned. "I might have known it."

3. "But nae doubt he'll coom back for this birdie, an' he can hae it, and welcome." "Oh, canny, mannie," smiled the other Mac, who saw the plot. "It occurs to me that it's not me that'll be blown up."

4. Then did the wicked MacHaggis get a worm, and tie it to a long, slow match. "Puir, sweet wee birdio!" he chuckled, "jeest get a wriggler into your gizzard, and dinna heed the string." "Ay," replied the cock-a-doodle: "I wilt."

5. Now MacWeedrap was on the watch, and directly he saw the rooster running round in a circle with a long line attached, he thought it'd get choked. "Come back, ye pesteeferous crow!" he yelled. "I mean to catch ye!"

6. Well, MacWeedrap caught more than he bargained for. At the precise moment that bird went BANG, and away went both. "Farewell, ma bonnie braw laddie!" yelled MacHaggis: "gi' my respects to the mon in the moon."

Illustrated Chips 509; 2 June 1900

SOME OF THE MYSTERIES OF LOAN AND DISCOUNT

1. As Iky Mo and ALLY SLOPER could raise no more money on their own account, what was more natural than that they should start a Loan Office, and lend money to others.

2. Iky began with a splendid notion: "Let's advertise Loans without the least inquiry or the slightest security."

3. And didn't the public respond?

4. Only ALLY's great idea of "Twopence for a form of application" didn't seem to answer.

5. "Capital, one million." View of the interior of the iron safe.

6. This is a "Meeting of the Board." SLOPER became personally acquainted. N.B.—*They had a would-be borrower's feet in them too at the time.*

7. And this is a faithful likeness of a pair of boots with which Mr.

Judy; 14 August 1867 (Marie Duval)

The Comic Hero

Alexander Sloper, F.O.M. (Friend of Man), was known as Ally for short and for good reason: fond of that quarter-day caper called the Moonlight Flit, he was forever sloping up an alley. Born on 14 August 1867, of mixed parentage (writer C. H. Ross, artist Marie Duval, Mrs Ross), he spent seventeen years in *Judy* strips before W. G. Baxter remodelled him for thirty-two more years as a cartoon in *Ally Sloper's Half-Holiday*. Here his hobnobbing with royalty reformed the 'Old Rumfoozler' as little as did his regular arrests by the peelers. If not the first ever comic strip hero, certainly the first ever anti-hero, Ally established the outlaw as everybody's favourite funmaker. More, he operated in tandem with Isaac (Iky) Moses (Mo), thus establishing the double act, too.

ARREST OF SLOPER.

*" A raid has been made on 'The Sloperies,' and Poor Papa has been arrested by the Police. Personally, I know very little of the matter; but, from what the Dook tells me, it appears that, for some time past, Mr. Moses has been conducting a Betting Club in one of the upstairs rooms at '99.' The Police are in no way to blame; the affair was forced upon them by the Home Secretary. There wasn't a dry eye amongst the Constables engaged, and the whole thing has caused a deep gloom throughout the Force. It is hoped, however, that 'ALLY SLOPER'S CHRISTMAS HOLIDAYS' will appear on the 8th, as already announced."—*TOOTSIE.

Ally Sloper's Half-Holiday 344; 29 November 1890 (W. F. Thomas)

½ ILLUSTRATED CHIPS 1D / 1D ½

No. 298.   Vol. XII. (New Series.)   [Entered at Stationers' Hall.]   PRICE ONE HALFPENNY.   [Transmission Abroad at Book Rates.]   May 16, 1896

INNOCENTS ON THE RIVER.

1. Weary Waddles : "I say, Timmy, a great idea has hit me in the head. If we catch that horse we can make him tow us in this boat."

2. Tired Timmy : "That's a noble scheme. You do the fancy work, and catch the animal."

3. W. W. "How's this? Ye'd take me for a Dragoone the Queen's Bodyguard, wouldn't ye?"

4. T. T. "Ah! this reminds me of the old days at Oxford. Have you the luncheon-basket, Willie?"

5. W. W. } "Great Pip! Bridge ahoy! Hi! Whoa—
T. T. } whoa, you brute!"

6. And then they got out and walked.

Illustrated Chips 298; 16 May 1896 (Tom Browne)

'He Knew How To Do It' was the title of Tom Browne's first published work, printed in James Henderson's comic *Scraps* on 27 April 1889. A significant title to a significant cartoon: an eight-panelled strip of slapstick paperhanging. Tom, born 1870, was a poor Nottingham apprentice, and the thirty shillings Henderson sent him was equal to three months' salary in the print shop. Tom answered Harmsworth's ad for artists and soon chucked up the litho trade for *Comic Cuts*. His 'Innocents on the River', just another set for *Chips*, caught the public's fancy, and 'Weary Waddles and Tired Timmy' soon took over the entire front page, slightly rechristened 'Weary Willy and Tired Tim' (p. 29). Tom modelled them on his own heroes, Don Quixote and Sancho Panza, and later turned them into a strip, too (p. 30). Disreputable double acts caught on. Tom's 'Airy Alf and Bouncing Billy' (p. 82), bicyclists (Tom's favourite pastime), soon turned tramp and even met their mirror-image rivals (p. 31). Footpads hit the front page highway in comic after comic.

MIXED THINKS

CHIPS FUNNY MAN

ILLUSTRATED
CHIPS
1d
2

No. 471. Vol. XVIII. (New Series.) [Entered at Stationers' Hall.] PRICE ONE HALFPENNY. [Transmission Abroad at Book Rates.] September 9, 1899.

A WILD NIGHT'S ADVENTURE WITH SPRING-HEELED JACK.

1. "Willy, dear boy, how do I strike you?" warbled Tim. "Strike me—throw me—pinch me—bust me! but you're just too wonderful for words!" smiled Willy. "Are you Spring-heeled Jack, or a winged microbe? Oh, I know now! You're the Human Bat what we read about in the 'Wonder.'"

2. And sure enough that vampire had a giddy time of it that evening on the common. "Wough! I am the ghost of your fat uncle!" roared the monster. "Don't run, children; let's stop and play together." "No you don't," roared the crowd, "we never had a uncle—at least, not with a dial like that! Ta-ta!"

3. So the Bat popped in to see how Sophie and Jack were getting on with their spooning. "Coughdrops and liver pills!" yelled the chap; "may I be stewed in hair-oil if it isn't the old 'un!" "Yow! Ho-oh! Hellup! Take it away!" twittered the maiden. "I'll never marry with anything like that in the family."

4. Once more across the common the Bat spotted a few of his old enemies. "Oh, you beauties!" he whistled. "I've got you now, and if I don't knock spots out of your earholes may I be sugared!" "Don't touch us, Mister Bat," yelled the cops; "we're too young to die."

5. But if the cops were nervous the night-birds weren't, and they flocked up to see what the row meant. "'Ere, what do you call yourself?" piped the old crow. "Let's have a taste!" Peck, peck! "Willy," shrieked Tim, "'ere are some nasty dicky-birds hurting your little pal."

6. Poor Willy was in too much of a tangle to go to the rescue, and presently a crowd of yokels came along with a gun and other hurtful instruments. "Come, birdie, come, and fly with me." snorted Tim, as they pitched him into the pond. "I am coming, gentle Timmy," whined Willy. Then the cold waters closed over them! But they'll appear, as per, in Chips next Thursday.

9/9/99

Illustrated Chips 471; 9 September 1899 (Tom Browne)

The Unrecorded Adventures of Don Quixote de Tintogs and Sancho Panza, His Faithful Servant.

INTRODUCTION.

NOW it is well known that Don Quixote was an old-fashioned gentleman who gave himself up so wholly to the reading of romances that a-nights he would pore on until day, and a-days he would read on until it was night; and thus, by sleeping little and reading much, the moisture of his brain was exhausted to that degree that at last he lost the use of his reason.

A world of disorderly notions, picked out of books, crowded into his imagination; and now his head was full of nothing but enchantments, quarrels, battles, challenges, wounds, complaints, amours, and abundance of stuff and impossibilities, insomuch that all the fables and fantastical tales which he read seemed to him now as true as the most authentic histories.

Having thus lost his understanding, he unluckily stumbled upon the oddest fancy that ever entered a madman's brain, even in a comic paper; for now he thought it necessary, as well for his own honour as the service of the public, to turn knight-errant, and roam through the whole world, armed cap-à-pie, and mounted on his steed, Rozinante, in quest of adventures.

The adventures of this remarkable person and his simple, faithful servant, Sancho Panza, have been related in a famous work, but it has been reserved for us to convey to the world the true narration of the exploits of these worthies as they really occurred, together with some spicy tales concerning Rozinante, the horse, the ass, and the entirely-forgotten dog, Trust, who will now appear for the first time. These adventures will appear (ONE EACH WEEK). We shall proceed to correct some existing delusions upon the best-known adventures of Don Quixote, and tell first—

THE TRUE STORY OF THE TOSSING IN THE BLANKET.

1. One day as the weary knight approached an inn he saw, to his astonishment, his servant, Sancho Panza, being tossed in a blanket. Filled with wrath, he bade them stop.

2. But as they took no notice, he hastily mounted his trusty steed (Rozinante, the catsmeat vendor's hope), but with the wrong leg up first.

3. Consequently, setting spurs to his trusty steed, he entered the yard in a not too dignified manner. "Put old Tintogs in as well," they cried.

4. And in he went into the blanket. Just then Sancho's ass strolled in. "In with the ass," they cried.

5. No sooner was the ass in the blanket when some-one cried, "In with the boneshaker."

6. So in went pussie's hope, followed by the dog, Trust, just for luck—tossing "heads and tails," as it were.

Comic Cuts 440; 15 October 1898 (Tom Browne)

Newsagents will find it pays them to display

The Big Budget. 1ᵈ

GRAND FOOTBALL SERIAL STORY
JUST STARTED.

VOL. V. No. 122.　　　WEEK ENDING SATURDAY, OCTOBER 14, 1899.　　　PRICE 1D.

AIRY ALF AND BOUNCING BILLY MEET THEIR GREAT RIVALS.

1. AIRY ALF and BOUNCING BILLY had blued all their coin, and were padding the hoof to the B.B. office, to knock a few bobs out of the Editor. "Billy," chirped Alf, "ole B.B.'s knocking 'em all with that noo football serial, ain't he?" And Billy was jist about to open his little potato-trap to reply when——

2. The rivals came face to face. "G-r-r!" gasped Weary Tim and Tired Willy. Is it them er their ghosts?" And the Budget boys gurgled: "Is it troo, or is it onli a nightmare?"

3. Then the first act of the tr-r-agedy commenced. "A-h-a!" hissed Tired Willy, as he biffed Billy neatly. "I've been wanting to talk to you for a long time." And Weary Tim sweetly purred: "Take that, you slab-sided son of a bottle-nosed slop."

4. You will observe, dear readers, that the argument is still proceeding. "Billy," gasped Alf, "how's our ride?" And Billy's voice arose from the scrimmage, and warbled: "Arf a mo, cooky. I'm jist tryin to git a bit of 'is ear orf."

5. At length youth began to tell. "Oh-er," gasped Weary Tim, who had got the worst of the knock-out. "I feel sorter run down." And Tired Willy chipped in: "I fink I've had enuff, Jockies. Let's play at sumfing else, shall we?"

6. The great battle was over, and the Budget boys were on top. "Alf, my nobel warrier," said Billy, "it was a good scrap, wasn't it?" "Get out," chortled the long 'un, "Why, arsk 'em wot they fink about it." And two mournful moans arose on the air, and voices groaned: "Let's 'ave one more gargle afore we die."

Big Budget 123; 14 October 1899 (Ralph Hodgson)

31

OUR COLOURED NUMBER LAST WEEK BROKE ALL RECORDS. — ANOTHER COMING SOON.

Comic Cuts. ½d.

ONE HUNDRED LAUGHS FOR A HALFPENNY.

No. 355. Vol. XIV.] REGISTERED. ONE HALFPENNY WEEKLY. [FEBRUARY 27, 1897.

CHOKEE BILL AND HIS NOOMATIC INJYRUBBER BOOTY-BAG (continued next week).

1. "Did I never tell yer nuffink abart me noomatic booty-bag, Mr. Edditter? No! Well, 'ere goes, then. Yer see, the cops had got yoosed ter me cawpit-bag, an' so me and Snaggums (the Skinny Kid) invented a noomatic injyrubber booty-bag, wot 'ud go in yer pocket, an' would stretch ter ercommodate any quantity of booty yer could collar.

2. "Yer'll 'awdly berlieve me, Mr. Edditter, but the werry fust bit o' swag I collared in that there booty-bag wos a private gemman, a watch-dorg, an' a perliceman. 'Ow did I do it! Well, like this 'ere. I'd just farstened me booty-bag onter a winder-ledge, so's I could drop me swag in froo the winder—

3. "When a dorg as I'd never noticed made a sudding honslaught onter me. In I bolts froo the winder.

4. "Fortchernetly, the dorg dropped a bit short, and fell whack inter me noomatic bag.

5. "But not before he'd wakened the pawty in the 'ouse wiv his barkin' an' 'owlin'. The conserquence wos, I had ter bolt for that winder again in a jiff, wiv the 'ouseholder an' a cop at me 'eels.

6. "In course I made a jump ter clear me noomatic booty-bag; but the 'ouseholder pawty, knowing nuffink abart it—

7. "Went a swatter into it, onter the poodle, wot wos a-whiskin' raand inside.

8. "Well, that wos a bit o' luck orlright; but when the cop comes an' stawts gittin' out backards way for safety, an' drops smack in onter the poodle an' the 'ouseholder pawty, I see'd me charnce; an' just as he dropped—

9. "I tied up the marth o' me injyrubber booty-bag and cavorted safe as 'ouses! Worn't it a corker?"

*23/2.97

Comic Cuts 355; 27 February 1897 (Frank Holland)

"The Terror of the Seas; OR, THE Mysteries of the Deep." SEE INSIDE.

The Funny Wonder

EVERY SATURDAY, 1d. 1/2

No. 268. Vol XI.   ONE HALFPENNY, EVERY SATURDAY.   MARCH 19, 1898.

AUBREY 'AWKINS AND GINGER JONES TRY TO NICK THE CROWN JEWELS.

1. Aubrey and Ginger were clean pebbly-stoney, as per, and being badly in want of a hundred thousand quid to buy toffee with, they thought they'd go to the Tower of London and sneak the crown jewels. "Ha! ha!" murmured Aubrey, as they got to the entrance; "but we must be wary!" "Wot ho!" said Ginger.

2. They managed to find their way up to the bedroom of the chap who had the keys, and Aubrey sprang at him like a cannon-ball with the jumps. "So ho, villin!" he yelled, "you are in our power, and must lead us to the room where the jools be!" "Yus; and look slippy," chipped in Ginger.

3. That yeoman of the guard, being an obliging chap, said he would. "'Tis well, caitiff. We will follow thee," said Aubrey. "Lead hon, Macduff!" grinned Ginger. "And look 'ere—no hurts!"

4. When they got to the Tower, Ginger thought he'd like to make the acquaintance of the cove in the meat-tin on horseback. But the chap didn't like being interfered with, and he nearly squashed the dinner out of the Auburn One. "Yoow! chuck it!" yelped Ginger. "You've tore my evenin' dress!"

5. At last they got to the Jewels Room, and Aubrey ordered the yeoman to do up as many of the valuables as they could carry in a brown-paper parcel. "Aub," cried Ginger, "wot price me? S'lute yer king, can't yer!" "Rats!" said Aubrey.

6. But they got sucked in after all; for that yeoman chap managed to give 'em the wrong parcel. "Don't think much of your jooller's shop," grinned Ginger, when they undid the parcel. "Which shall we sell first—the Royal Diamond Cat or the Himperial Golden Dog?" (They don't seem to have much luck, do they?—Ed.)

10/3/98

The Funny Wonder 268; 19 March 1898

OGDEN'S "TAB" CIGARETTES IN PENNY PACKETS CONTAINING 5.

"HOW I CONDUCTED A PET'S PARADISE" Will Tickle You.

THE World's Comic. 1d 2

EDITED BY JOHN JOLLYBOY

A WEEK'S LAUGHTER FOR ONE HALFPENNY.

No. 295. Vol. XII.] Registered.   ONE HALFPENNY WEEKLY.   [February 23, 1898.

BAT-EARED BILL AND MOOCHING MIKE START A CAT'S MEAT ROUND.

1.—Tuesdays and Fridays was their day for the cat's meat fake, so they fixed up the old pram with a mysterious box atop. "Ah! stock meat's werry low, pardner, we'll 'ave ter get more stuff."

2.—But they didn't sell a ha'p'orth—they just chucked free lunches around till the street was alive with cats and dogs. What was their little game? Wait and you will see.

3.—"Look spry! Mick, me pippen," gurgled Bill, "we've just got room for 'arf-a-dozen more. Snick that poodle if yer gets 'arf a chance."

4.—Then they made tracks for the Country Sausage Factory, Isle o' Dogs, not forgetting the mysterious box and all.

5.—On the next round Bat-eared Bill and Mooching Mike got hawking cheap sausage till a wild-looking gent wanted to know how his missin' dog's collar got inside last week's lot.

6.—Then the mob rolled up, smashed the barrer, and started to lynch the firm. Fortunately a bobby took charge of 'em, and invited 'em to lunch with him at the police-station. More howling adventures to come.

HOW I CONDUCTED
A PET'S PARADISE.

"Cat Homes are common enough, perhaps," I remarked to a man, whose nose testified eloquently to indigestion or strong drink, "but my repository for four-legged aristocracy was a decided curiosity. It was a 'Hydropathic for superior domestic animals,' as my prospectus modestly had it, 'where the dear animals—be they tabby or bull-dog—will be treated on a scale of magnificence never before attempted by rival institutions!'

Of course many funny-minded people laughed hugely at the way I expressed things, but I didn't mind their sarcastic mirth—they weren't likely to put a penny my way in any case. More important was the fact that thousands of maiden ladies perused my circulars—for I had issued them with great discrimination—and hugged their darling "Fidos" and "Purrikins" as they pictured the delightful retreat for their pets when afflicted with the dulls.

I secured a jerry-built suburban villa which, though of very modest dimensions and rent, called for immense respect under the breezy name of "Mount Azone." To this mansion I earnestly requested intending patrons to enrol as members at once, before, by stress of numbers, their applications would have to be refused. On the second day letters began to dribble in, and by next day they had formed a delightful pile. There was one with a coronet in sky blue, over which I gloated before desecrating the envelope.

"Countess ———,"—so began the delicately-perfumed epistle—"requests that Professor Du Blanqu" (that was myself) "will call and afford her information of his Hydropathic for Dogs, at 8.30 to-night."

"With the utmost pleasure, my dear Countess," I breathed, touching the tender part of my nose with the embossed arms to make sure that I wasn't dreaming.

In appropriate toggery, which fitted me admirably for hired goods, I had an interview with the Countess. Her ladyship was going on a tour to the Better Land or the Holy Land, I forget which. Was I sure I could suitably entertain her dog "Nebuchadnezzar," who had been professionally appraised at £495 and some coppers? I assured my titled patroness that he'd be an honoured guest, even superseding in my estimation the poodle pup belonging to a certain Duchess, which I was bringing up on the bottle. I left, promising to

The World's Comic 295; 23 February 1898

NOTICE TO ERRAND BOYS! TRY FOR ONE OF THE "WORLD'S COMIC" MONEY PRIZES.

FUNNY ½d CUTS

EDITED BY GORDON PHILLIP HOOD.

The Monday Edition of this paper is called the WORLD'S COMIC. Don't forget to buy one.

No. 404. Vol. XVI.] Registered.   ONE HALFPENNY WEEKLY.   [April 2, 1898.

THE THREE BEERY BOUNDERS AND THE BIG BALLOON (continued).

1.—"More larks!" cries Fly Flipper; "we'll give this chap a bit of a lift, if I can manage to switch on."

2.—And wasn't that poor pedal pusher surprised when he found his bike had taken it into its head to fly.

3.—But he held on to the handle bar until Nosey knocked him off with a sand-bag, then the Beery ones hauled in the bike. "We're doing well," says Fatty.

4.—The next thing they tried to lift was a horse and cart. Then the trouble commenced.
"Strikes me that'll be a bit 'eavy," says Nosey.

5.—And Nosey was right. The balloon couldn't get away with it at all, and almost stood still.
"We're gonners," says Nosey, when he saw a man appear at a top storey window and commence to blaze away at the balloon with his gun.

6.—Down came the big balloon, and the Beery Bounders with it, slap into the middle of a river.
"A watery grave arter all!" gurgled Flipper. But they were rescued at the last moment, and the Three Beery ones are sure to be in another scrape next week.

Funny Cuts 404; 2 April 1898

HENRY T. JOHNSON'S GREAT STORY, "DANDY JIM." (SEE PAGE 2.)

THE 1½d Coloured Comic. 1½d

No. 1. Vol. I.]   ONE HALFPENNY.   [MAY 21, 1898.

OF THE SAME OPINION.

HOW FROG-FACED FERDINAND AND WATTY WOOL WHISKERS GOT A MONKEY.

(1) It was this way. The sailor left his box outside the pub and Frog-faced Ferdinand and Watty Wool Whiskers couldn't resist it, they really couldn't, you know. So they pinched it.

(2) And took it home and opened it, when—"Jumping Johnson!" out sprang a monkey, and after tickling Watty in the tater trap, it tried to pull his whiskers.

(3) Then it went for Ferdinand, and tried to pick his pocket in quite a professional style, which fairly won Watty's heart.

(4) "Good old Monkey Brand," shrieked Watty, "yer one o' the boys. Come ter me arms me long lost brother!"

(5) Then they thought they'd take a stroll and faked the monkey up in the landlady's togs. "Looks spiffing," says Froggy. "Only wants a veil," says Whiskers.

(6) In the park they met a masher. "Strike me spicey," says Wool Whiskers, "if he ain't mashed on the monkey. We oughter make toes out o' this."

(7) And that merry monkey kept it up, and managed to pinch the masher's watch, while Froggy pinched his wipe.

(8) Then the masher stole a ki— whiskers," he yelled, in dismay that settled him, and didn'

This is a Pippin, and no error. We all like it—so will you.

1. That gentleman guffing away there is Signor Alberto Bounderi, with his celebrated phonograph. Hist! dear readers, you recognise him? Well, don't blow the gaff then. "Walk up, ladies and gents," he shouts, "yer just about to 'ave the greatest treat of the season. Me famous funnygraph is now a-going to yap out a few select hairs, the same which it 'as performed before the German Emperor and all the corned feet of Europe. No coppers taken, and silver sniffed at. Walk up."

2. "'Ere you have the 'Soldiers of the Queen,' as sung by the Hero of Mafeking himself. 'Ark to the lovely notes of that magnificent barrowtone voice." "It's a fair coughdrop," shouted the crowd, and the pieces began to dribble in. "Well, this looks like a bit of sugar for the bird," chortled Bertie Bounder, "wot price kippers for breakfast termorrow?"

3. When the phonograph started reciting the Charge of the Light Brigade, the enthusiasm was immense, and the spondulicks simply poured in. "My eye," crooned Bertie to himself, as he gazed before the delighted crowd, "this beats a whelk stall all hollow." But, unfortunately, he did not notice that nasty inquisitive sailor man at the back. "I wonder 'ow them funnygraphs work. I've a great mind to just lift this one up and——"

4. And just as Bertie was wallowing in the little quidlets, with his back towards the phonograph, the sailor lifted the top off the machine, and—gave the whole show away; for 'twas Algy a-working that funnygraph all on his own. "You now get the chance of a lifetime, people," cooed Bertie, as he stuffed the oof into his pockets, "to 'ear the lovely voice of the most beyootiful singer of the present day——" "You bloomin' frauds," howled the crowd, "we'll goffer yer."

5. And then the crowd took them to the end of the pier, and gave them a nasty, rude, rough push into the cold, kerewel sea. "Oh, save me," screamed Algy, "save yer boyhood's pal. I'm delicate, I shall be sure to die if I get drownded. Oh, why don't somebody throw me a lifebelt." "'Elp," shrieked Bertie, "man overboard. Take yer dirty boots out o' me weskit."

6. Fortunately, the mud wasn't very deep just there, and so they managed to get ashore, and made tracks for the station, with the crowd full pelt after them. "Bertie," puffed Algy, "they're catching us up. Why didn't yer listen ter me when I told yer ter keep honest?" "Rats!" panted Bertie. "It's you wot's the cause of orl my troubles."

Big Budget 161; 14 July 1900 (Charles Genge)

1. DEER MISTER EDDITTER,—We wos burgl'n'. I know it wos norty, but we wos doin' it. Jimmer 'ad worn his trotter-boxes darn till there wos 'ardly ennythink left of 'em but the lace-'oles, an' there wos nutthink for it— 'e 'ad ter 'ave a noo pare of 'oof-cases some'ow. So we busts inter a boot-shop. Well, we'd 'arily got nicely in when a cop spots us an' meks for the winder ter koller us.

2. "Spooky," ses Jimmer, "we're lorst!" "Lorst be 'anged," I ses. "You lose yer face! I've got a little wheeze wot'll worry that cop a bit. Wot we wornt is cover, a.n't it?" "Yus," ses Jimmer. "Well," I ses, "wot price this 'ere boot?" "Spooky," ses Jimmer, "geenius ain't the word fer you. You're a korf-drop." "Never mind wot I am or wot I ain't," I ses, "you foller me."

3. "Right o!" ses Jimmer: an' in 'arf a tick we wos tucked inside that boot as nice an' comfy as if we wos in a third class kerridge on a Bank 'ollerdy excurshun. "Sh-sh-sh-sh! 'ere's the cop; don't breave," ses Jimmer. "I can't," I ses, "yer squeedgin' too mutch." Then the cop garsps "lost, gorn? ¡Gorn? Well, this is the narstiest knock I've ever 'ad!" "I'd giv yer a narstier if I 'ad a brick," I wispers.

4. Then 'e blinks up an' darn, an' every time he looks up we ducks darn inter the boot. At larst 'e guv it up an' crorled orf. "I thort 'e wos goin' ter 'ave a fit," ses Jimmer, larfin'. "So 'e is," I ses. "An' a reglar parrelettic one too. Darn yer, git art of 'ere, Jimmer! Look slick! Now un'ook that boot! That's it!" An' in a cupple o' ticks, Mister Edditter, we 'ad that boot orf its 'inges, an' wos reddy for bizness.

5. "Wot's the game now, Spooky?" ses Jimmer, fairly flabbergarsted. "That's the game," I ses, pointin' to the copper darn below. "An' mind yer sees as yer pots him properly." Just then we 'ears the peeler murmurin' "Well, I dunno wot's a-comin' over me." "No," I ses, "but I know wot's a-comin' over yer—this," an' we drops the boot.

6. "Well, yer sed as yer'd give 'im a fit, Spooky," ses Jimmer, "an' I reckon you've guv 'im a booty." "Yus," I ses, "'e might ha' bin measured fer that boot, mightn't 'e?" An' after that we does our little bit o' bizness an' clears art. But yer shul ha' heerd the langwidge wot wos a-buzzin' inside that boot, Mister Edditter. It wos orful. Well, as I sed ter Jimmer, "Jimmer," I ses, "I can't stay 'ere an' listen to it. We must go." So we went.—Yoorstrooly, SPOOKY THE SPRAT.

Big Budget 176; 27 October 1900 (Frank Holland)

1. DEAR MISTER EDDITTER,—We've 'ad a werry near go this lawst week! We wos in the country for 'ealth an' rekerryation (an' ennyfink else we cud lay our 'ands on), an' wos just trottin' orf wiv a foo turmuts when the farmer an' a cop cums bunkin' arfter us.

2. There's no dowt we'd ha' bin kollered too, if we 'ad'nt suddingly cum to a wire fence, when I struck the idea o' yoosin' it as a kattypult, wiv the turmuts for hammynition (as per picter).

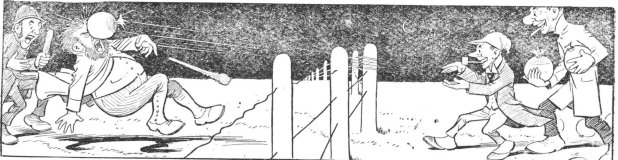

3. "Gimme me my turmuts!" yells the farmer, as 'e cums bouncin' up. "Right o! There yer are!" I ses, an' I biffs 'im wiv a big 'un right on the boco.

4. Over 'e goes, an' up cums the cop. "'And over them turmuts," 'e owls.

5. "Suttingly, yer lawdship," I ses, an' I 'ands 'im one on 'is chivvy, an' 'e flops over wivout so much as sayin', "Thenk yer."

6. O' coarse arfter that evveryfink wos orlright, and orf we toddled

Yours truly, SPOOKY THE SPRAT.

Big Budget 179; 17 November 1900 (Frank Holland)

1. "See here," said Hiram B. Boss to the City man, "there's buried treasure in your back garden at home—£10,000 of it. Gimme a cheque for £500, and I'll give you the plan. I've got ter catch a train."

"Ha-ha! not me," laughed the City man.

2. Hiram saw he was not to be had. "I rather calculate I'll have to make it a bit easier for him," he murmured. So he bought about five bobs' worth of brass counters, and buried them in that chap's back garden.

But he was observed.

3. And presently, two imps of boys came and dug up the box with those counters, and took it away, and in its place put a box they had borrowed from their little brother, who was away from home.

4. The next time Hiram turned up in that City man's office, he said: "See, I'm back again! I missed that train; but if you'll promise me the £500 the minute I shows you the gold, I'll take yer to yer condemned garden and hold the lantern while yer digs it."

"That's better," said the City man. "Have a cigar."

5. "Ho, ho!" said the City man, "the gold, the gold, the red, red gold!" when he dug up the box.

"Got that £500 in notes?" said Hiram.

"I've only got to undo the catch," went on the City man, "and wealth is mine, beyond the dream of a policeman!"

6. But it wasn't wealth he got. No; it was a nasty, ugly, little Jack jumper which the imps had borrowed from their little brother.

My! didn't Hiram have a happy, happy time!

The Funny Wonder 259; 15 January 1898 (Jack B. Yeats)

EPHRIAM BROADBEAMER

SMUGGLER PIRATE AND OTHER THINGS

1. A terrible storm was raging at Ephriam's birthplace, and the townspeople were alarmed for the safety of the boats. "Only one thing for it!" yelled Ephriam to the Mayor. "Pour oil on the troubled water."

2. The Mayor happened to be an oil-merchant, and so he took Ephriam's tip, and altogether they spilt about a thousand gallons on the waves. It had the desired effect, though.

3. And that was where Ephriam came in. As soon as the oilers had cleared off, he scooted down to the beach, got his boat, and scooped in gallon after gallon of the oil, for, as you know, oil always floats at the top of water.

4. He made a good bit out of it; but, of course, he must needs go and spoil himself by being greedy. He hadn't got enough to satisfy himself, so he went up to the Mayor again. "There's another storm a-comin', and we wants more oil," he said. He didn't get it—the Mayor had been watching him.

The Funny Wonder 284; 7 July 1898 (Jack B. Yeats)

Jack B. Yeats' style was as different from Tom Browne and his school as his crooks were from Tom's tramps. Perhaps this might be expected of the son of a poet (William Butler Yeats). Like Browne, Yeats later turned away from the black linework of comics to the coloured brushwork of paintings; unlike Browne, Yeats was never imitated. His artistry stands alone in British comics. 'Hiram B. Boss' and 'Ephraim Broadbeamer' are clearly unique crooks, just as his 'Chubb-Lock Homes' (p. 45) is out of the ruck of comic coppers—traditional game in the Victorian comic, traditional game today. Comic editors often appeared as comic heroes (p. 46) or guest stars (pp. 47–8); proprietors, too (p. 17).

No. 34. Vol. II.] Registered   ONE HALFPENNY WEEKLY.   [FEBRUARY 28, 1891.

THE SWADDY, THE SLAVEY, AND THE SLOP.

I.—Coogy and the Parrot were At Home to their pet Policeman, but just when the cold mutton was about to tighten his belt——

II.—Horror of horrors! a Guardsman's shadow darkened the windy blind. "Oh, lor, Robert, if 'taint my cousin Dick," shrieked the fair but frail Cook. "Inter the pantry, quick.'

III —It was all very well; but, Jerusalem, worn't it a squeeze; they just managed it in time, though, and that's all.

IV.—All went well till that wretched Parrot up and opened his mouth with one fatal speech !!!

V.—The son of Mars went for that cupboard straight; and a good deal of fur and feather started flying around.

VI —They went at it like catamounts till they collected the bits which belonged to 'em, and got them gone. They haven't called on that fickle-hearted Cooky since; not much !!!

Funny Cuts 34; 28 February 1891 (Alfred Gray)

Funny Cuts 41; 18 April 1891 (Alfred Gray)

1. "I SAY! dem perlice fellys is after me yet. It got so hot I had ter drop me bag of gold wot I took 'ast week. But watch me in me submarine 'dug-out,' wot I nicked from de French. But look! One 'o dem cops is shootin'! I'll just git in an' touch de 'goin' souf' button. Bullits is bullits."

2. Chorus of P.C.'s: "Well I'm blanketty blanketted! An' just wen glorious victoriousn was ours. Well, anyway, we've one consolation, we got that bag of gold back. Where the b. summonses is he?"

3. THE KID: "Hush! nor a word! I've cum up on dis side. See? And dis bag of stuff won't hurt me a bit!" And Brains, the dog, said: "Bless me noo 'at, I dursn't breathe. Quick I'll bust."

4. Chorus: "Great Scott! He was at this side now. He carn't stop down long for want airy atmosphere. Next time we nab him, sure! And then—ah!"

5. But no. It was not to be that time for he came up in the middle with a mighty swooshter. And Brains said: "Capital, it's a bull's-eye!"

6. And when the big moon arose, the Kid, on the upper deck, said: "How many hats cou thou, Brains, not countin' the fish?" "Six, me noble lord," answered Brains. "T'is w one mighty strike we have turned the whole of the B.B. division into food for fishes." An fish said: "Thanks, admiral, since you remind me. I'll go an' 'ave a mouthful." And he

Big Budget 96; 15 April 1899 (Frank Wilkinson)

The Funny Wonder 1d ½

THE SATURDAY EDITION OF "COMIC CUTS."

No. 219. VOL. IX. [NEW SERIES.]   ONE HALFPENNY WEEKLY.   APRIL 10, 1897.

ADVENTURES OF CHUBBLOCK HOMES AND SHIRK, THE DOG DETECTIVE.

1. Chubblock Homes, the great detective, had hunted everything, from gamps to lost hearts, but he never hunted little pet pigs before. "Find him!—our Adolph—our little curly-tailed cherub—and great rewards are yours! That's his picter; let Shirk sniff it!" So said the guardian of Adolph, the Baby Pig.

2. The chase began. What is yonder sign? Ham is cheap. Alas! poor Adolph. "On, on! let us hear the wust!" gurgled the guardian down in his slippers.

3. "No, no!" said the ham-and-beef man, "I have not cooked your little Adolph; but I saw a man go by with him towards the dog show." That was enough. On went Chubblock Homes and Shirk. The owner of Adolph was tired; so he rode.

4. At the dog show. The robbers had escaped with Adolph; but an artist for a daily paper had made a sketch of the little pet. The judges had thought he was a foreign pug dog, and given him first prize. Shirk, upsetting the owner of the pig, took a good sniff at the drawing. Then the chase was resumed—

5. Hallo! a lot of ladies fighting. "Say," cried Chubblock Homes, "tell me, young man in the button, what is the cause of yonder battle?" "Oh, it's only the mothers fighting over the way the first prize went in the baby show." Oho! the baby show. A suspicion flashes through Chubblock's mind.

6. The way the first prize went—it went to little Adolph. They thought the petsie, ducksie, ickle sing was a baby. But the thief escaped, taking those prizes with him.

The Funny Wonder 219; 10 April 1897 (Jack B. Yeats)

The Funny Wonder

1d ½

No. 246. Vol. XI
ONE HALFPENNY, EVERY SATURDAY.
OCTOBER 16, 1897,

OUR EDITOR'S ADVENTURES AS A BURGLAR.

1. Mr. Comic Cuts was sick and tired of cautioning the servant against leaving the windows open at night. It was no use; she would do it.

2. So our Editor thought he would give her a fright, which would prove a useful lesson to her. He disguised himself as a burglar—all complete, just like Chokee Bill.

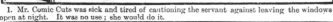

3. Then he climbed through the kitchen-window, chuckling to himself. But there was a surprise in store for him. The parrot spotted him, and gave the alarm.

4. And Martha, the servant, being strong-minded, simply went for our poor Editor like a hurricane. "Go it, Martha!" cried the parrot, and Martha went it strong.

5. Mrs. Comic Cuts, hearing the noise, came in and sat on "the burglar" while Martha went for the police. The police arrived, and then—

6. Mr. Comic Cuts sat up. Then his wife saw who it was. So did the parrot. So did Martha. Mr. Comic Cuts will never play burglar again.

The Funny Wonder 246; 16 October 1897 (A. H. Clarke)

Wonderful new | SPLENDID 100TH NUMBER. | Competition starts

The Big Budget. 1d

Are you reading "Caged," the romance of a lunatic asylum, in PEARSON'S WEEKLY? Just commenced.

VOL. IV. No. 100.   WEEK ENDING SATURDAY, MAY 13, 1899.   PRICE 1D.

AIRY ALF AND BOUNCING BILLY ROOK THE BIG BUDGET EDITOR.

1. It was like this. On the great er-casion of the 100th number of t'e old B.B., Airy Alf and Bouncing Billy asked the B.B. Editor to give 'em a look up. And old B.B, of course, was only too delighted. Here he is going in.

2. Inside Billy made his great speech. "Nobel Chief," he warbled, with tear-shaken voice. "Hon thee behalf ov arf a million grateful readers. We give you greeting. 'Tis 100 weeks sints you mai l the old emispear ring like a bad 'arf-dollar. 'Tis——" But Alf whispered: "Shuttup, ole gaspipe, and get the presents out."

3. Then out came t'e little tokens from Airy Alf. "Take 'em, me jipp'n," murmured Alfie. "I got 'em cheap at a sale." But look at Billy. Why, if he ain't borrowing old B.B.'s handkerchief.

4. It was Bil's turn after this. "You will hobserve," he murmured, "that the clock winds hup at the back, and the bull-pup's licence is in 'is left-hand earhole." And old B.B. was too full for words.

5. "What a fine thing it is," whispered the Budget Boss, "to have such kind, generous, thoughtful friends. Those nuggets'll come in very handy to pay this quarter's rent." And Alf whispered to Billy: "Let's go and see how the cricket's getting on."

6. Hit us with a hard brick, gentle reader. We must be sleeping. But no—it was no dream. "If you don't pay hup this bill immedi't hon the spot," sed the man with the club, "I'll b—— yer into nothingness." And so old B.B. had to part up. He s looking for that new hat—to say nothing of the hat and stick); and when he meets these two—well, just wait till he does.

Big Budget 100; 13 May 1899 (Ralph Hodgson)

47

JUST OUT!

No. 1.

TWELVE PAGES.

EVERY WEDNESDAY.

THE HALFPENNY COMIC 1/2 1D

No. 1, Vol. I.   SATURDAY, JAN. 22, 1898.   ONE HALFPENNY.

THE ADVENTURES OF MR. STANLEY DEADSTONE AND COMPANY.

(1) The Editor thinks of a grand idea. He will get his old friend, Mr. Stanley Deadstone, the explorer, to describe his adventures in the East on his own page.

(2) The Editor interviews Mr. S. D., who, since his return from Africa some months ago, has been playing the deuce with himself.

(3) The Editor tells Mr. S. D. what he wants. The explorer says he will roam all over the earth in search of adventures. Editor : "And don't touch a drop of whisky until you have left England." "Norrabit, old chap." Goes away.

(4) Meets his old friends, Ananias Canard and Longbow Fibber. Tells of his commission. They go and drink success to his expedition, until they get a bit lively by eleven o'clock at night.

(5) The three friends, arm-in-arm, proceed towards St. Paul's, yelling out "Should Auld Acquaintance," much to the disgust of the inhabitants of the houses.

(6) They get wild, upset a roast chestnut stand, and after a fight with the owner of the stand, two policemen arrive and run them all in.

"Jack Ahoy!" a thrilling story of adventure, by Henry T. Johnson, begins on the next page.

The Halfpenny Comic 1 ; 22 January 1898 (Tom Browne)

48

1. "Deer Sir,—I'm that mad I could eat Hezekiah Spudkins raw. Arter all 'e did ter me larst week me heart wos softened terwards 'im cos the parson come an' torked that evenin' abart brotherly love an' sich. Arter a tremenjous struggle wi' meself (which I'm 'avin in this picter), I ses 'I'll forgive him.'

2. "An' I goes right out, an', puttin' me dooks out, 'Hezekiah,' I ses, 'gimme yer 'and, an' from now let us be brothers!' Well, at that he was quite took back. 'Balmpot, old boy,' 'e ses, arter 'e'd done bein' took back, 'I will.'

3. "An' as 'e gripped my dook we both turned away an' swollered summat in our throats—lumps they wos. 'An' now,' I ses, as me voice shook, 'let all be forgotten. Wotever blaggardly treatment I've received from you, Hezekiah, I forgives.'

4. "'Blaggardly treatment?' 'e ses, sudden. 'I ain't aware, Augustus, as I was ever gilty of any sich!' Worn't that paltry, Mr. Edditer, after my 'andsome treatment of 'im?

5. "'Then I'm a liar, am I?' I ses, my dander risin'. 'You insultin' scoundrel, I'll gouge yer eye out!' 'You'll wot?' he says. 'Dare to, an' I'll——'

6. "'You dare me, do you, you villainous brute! I'll grind you to pulp!' I ses.

7. "An' wiv me British blood fairly up, sir, I flew at 'im, an' scratched an' bit 'im like a wild cat.

8. "An' if the perlice 'adn't interfered, sir, I'd 'ave shown 'im the stuff I wos made of, if I'd 'ad to chaw 'im up to do it.—Yoors trooly,
AUGUSTUS BALMPOT."

The Funny Wonder 259; 15 January 1898 (Frank Holland)

MR. BODGER PUTS IN A PANE OF GLASS.

1. "We'll soon have this new pane of glass in, my dear," said Mr. Bodger. "No need to have a glazier blundering about the house over a little job like that. You see, we just chop out the old glass and putty—

2. "Then we take the new pane of glass—so, and put it in!"

3. But instead of fitting it in, Mr. Bodger pushed it right through, and it fell out into the street.

4. And, as luck would have it, it dropped on the head of Beery Benjamin.

5. Beery Benjamin couldn't miss a chance like that. In about two-fifths of a second he was inside Bodger's house demanding compensation.

6. And Mr. Bodger had to pay. And, what's more, he gave that window-mending to a glazier after all!

The Funny Wonder 255; 18 December 1897 (S. W. Cavenagh)

1. "Make me a glass optic," said the one-eyed party; and the Handy Man said "Right!"

2. "Well," says the Handy Man, "first I tried a red-blue-and-green glass marble; but he said it was too fancy for him. Jist then my eye dropped on my ole telescoop. So I says, 'Whacher think of a telescopic eye?'

3. "Well, first I redooces the size of my ole telescoop. It took a lot of redoocing with the meat-chopper; but I thought if I got a fiver for the job it 'ud be wuth it.

4. "Then I fixed it in the ole party's empty skylight, and proceeded to paint an eye on the end just like Nater, only more. I had to tie up the ole 'un dooring the continuance of the proceedings.

5. "But at last it was done. and the party, having paid me, clutched hold of my arm and said, 'This is all right! Come and see it work. Observe yonder fishwife.' I observed.

6. "Well, he went up to her, and, 'Is that sole fresh?' says he. 'I have me doubts.' 'By Axelander Pip!' says the fishwife, 'is it fresh? There ain't nothink fresher in the entire ocean!' Then the old party touched the spring, and—

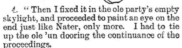

7. "Let go the telescopic eye, remarking at the same time, 'G-u-r-rh! You wicked story!' Well, it gave the ole fish-party such a turn that, if you ask her if her fish are fresh now, she tells you the exact day last week when they came out of the sea. Fact!"

The Funny Wonder 244; 2 October 1897 (Jack B. Yeats)

Falls and fights are the basis of slapstick, and 'The Spudkins-Balmpot Feud' celebrated nothing but knockabout for weeks on end. Domestic slapstick featuring father was frequent, and first regularised in the weekly adventures of 'Mr Bodger'. Jack Yeats' 'Handy Man' was less helpless, as you might have expected, and A. H. Clarke's 'Wimble' (p. 52) took on a new job every week. Tom Browne widened his horizon with 'Robinson Crusoe Esq' (p. 53); while Charles Genge pinned down a popular type in his 'Bertie Bounder' (p. 54).

The Halfpenny Comic ½

No. 65. Vol. III.]   WEEK ENDING APRIL 15, 1899.   [ONE HALFPENNY.

WIMBLES'S REMINOOSANCES.

1.—Ho no! It ain't orl sticky toffee bein' a railway hofficial. Frinstance, arter a little amoosement sech as the above, cultivatin' a tenpenny thirst on yer, the party sez "Thanks, o, so much! Take a track! We shall be offly appy to see yer at our little tin chapel on Sundays." And yer can only gurgle: "D'lighted, m'sure," cos yer too dry to say more.

2.—And then there's the old gel wot never couldn't even travel ter the next station without her menagerie, an' sez: "Dear me, Mister Porter, 'ow the little dears do take to yer! Ow remarkable it is that the little creechers can tell people wot is fond of em." Grrrh! A battered brown fer this lot, wot yer carn't even impoge on a aumakatic machine.

3.—And then the luggage orfis: people comes in and leaves things while they goes for ter set their watches. One of 'em left a thoughtful-lookin' dorg wot yer wouldn't suspect ennything wuss than chasing cats, an me, innercent like, labels 'im as per usual and leaves 'im with the other bundles.

4.—But, bless yer! When e opens the door agen, except a few odd bits, there weren't nothing but dorg left—not a sign of ennything else. So ter satisfy the people, I tries to work out by jography wot part of the dorg wos golfsticks and wot part wos washin' but not bein' a Solomon, I 'ad ter give it up and let 'em settle it peaceably amongst themselves.

5.—Which they wos bizzy doin', when the two thirty hup hexpress comes rattlin' along the metals, and I suddenly spots a hobstacle on the line, which pruved to be a brars button. Heedless of the danger to myself, I jumps down ter remove it—

6.—But alas, too late! an' I got such a uncommon tidy bump on a most wery inconvenient portion, it give me sech a earache I wos obliged to resign my position. (NEXT WEDNESDAY, WIMBLES AS A GARDENER.)

The Halfpenny Comic 65; 15 April 1899 (A. H. Clarke)

½d. ComicCuts. ½d.

ONE HUNDRED LAUGHS FOR A HALFPENNY.

No. 484. Vol. XIX.] Registered.　　ONE HALFPENNY WEEKLY.　　[August 19, 1899.

THE COMIC ADVENTURES OF ROBINSON CRUSOE, ESQUIRE, AND HIS MAN FRIDAY.
Poor Old Robinson Crusoe—in Luck Once Again.

1. You almost lost little Robbie last week, readers—you did, straight. You see, I was out with me own trew love and the rest of me family, when all of a suddint something with a Face—and *sich* a face—comes up out of the sea. "Yeeow!" remarks Mrs. C., "'tis me first 'usband come back from the ger-rave!" And then she deaded herself a bit. "Hellup!" I roared. "Mr. Serpint, I can recommend the cockles just the other side of the pier. You go and see if they ain't just *all* right."

2. But that serpint warn't no gentleman. He wouldn't take my advice—seemed to prefer to take me and my limited company for a little stroll. I wasn't frightened—oh! no. You can see that, can't you? But you ought to have heard old Payday—beg pardon, Friday—yelp. "Murder!" he howls. "Me auntie's making girdle-cakes, and she wants me. Hellup!"

3. And help came, it did. The Berritish Navy came to the rescue of yer pretty pal. "For," says the orficer of the gunboat, "if we let that there serpint carry off Robbie, what's going to become of Comic Cuts?" And echo answered "Wot?" "How's yer head?" he asks of the chap with the gun. "Bald!" says the chap. "Well, one, two, three—

4. "Fire!" And the chap fired. Of course I wasn't afraid not even then, but Friday—oh! Friday makes me disgusted. "Oh! why don't somebody save a poor nigger?" he howls. "I ain't done nobody no harm 'cept forty policemen and a sausage. Oh! Yo-o-o-o!" And that gun—oh! it did make a draught.

5. In fact it draughted so much that it blew us right on the beach—just by little Primrose (my wife by marriage). "So you've come back," says she, fierce-like. "Ye-es, me darling little eggshell," I said. "I've just been to get a breath of fresh air, and I *got all I wanted!*"

6. But there's no such thing as gratitude in this world. You'd have thought the missus would have been glad to get me back. But no! She had me run in for trying to desert her, and now I've got to do seven days' hard. Weep for us, will you?—Your own, Robinson.

Comic Cuts 484; 19 August 1899 (Tom Browne)

1. BERTIE BOUNDER took Flo and Gertie up the river the other day. Fair dook was Bertie, leaning back in the punt, with his arm round one girl, while the other did the work. The two tired, hot chaps on the bank looked longingly at the punt. "Wot-ho! fatheads!" shouted Bertie quite rudely, "don't yer wish yer was rich and good-looking like me? Don't wear yer boots out too fast walking, cockies."

2. Then when they got out at the Swagger Hotel, the two chaps came up and looked over the fence, and Bertie got ruder still: "Hullo, not dead yet," he chaffed, "wy dontcher come in, have lunch—ain't yer got any ooftish? Ha, ha!"

3. But while Bertie was enjoying himself with the girls, the two chaps thought they'd get their own back, and they moved that notice board and put it just where it would lead Bertie nicely over the weir. "Whoa, there," growled the fat chap, "yer a-shoving me into the river, stoopid!" However, they fixed the board up all right.

4. And when the punt came along, it was Bertie this time who was guiding the noble bark. "Ow," he yapped, as he saw the board, "good job I saw that board, girls, or I should have gone the other way for cert. You trust yerselves to me, dears, and you'll be all——"

5. Wallop! Sp'ash! Whish! They had reached the weir! Then the two heroes rushed out and nobly rescued the girls. "Saved, saved, darlings!" they chortled. "Cling to us," and the girls clung. "Oh, why don't somebody save me!" gurgled a voice from the bottom of the river (it was Bertie). "Save yerself," the two chaps laughed rudely, "you weren't born to be drownded."

6. And when Bertie finally crawled out, the girls were in the punt with those two chaps. "Go 'ome and get yerself wrung out!" the rude fellows sniggered, "we'll look after the girls." And Bertie limped off. (Look out for his last adventure next week. It is a funny one).

Big Budget 114; 19 August 1899 (Charles Genge)

The Comic Kid

Kids and comics were inseparable from the very beginning. Comics, intended for the working-class clerk and artisan, appealed to children because of their visual nature. Now and then editors slipped in 'Something for the Children': Tom Browne's 'Billy Buster the Steam Engine' in *Comic Cuts* for 14 March 1896, was described as 'a tale of a toy engine to be read aloud to the youngsters while they look at the pictures'. When children first appeared in comics, naturally it was as mischief-makers (p. 56). The first child heroes were, of course, as delinquent as their adult equivalents. Gordon Fraser's 'Ball's Pond Banditti' (p. 57) are the great grandfathers of 'Lord Snooty and His Pals', as their names testify: Ticko Scubbins, Gorger Pain, Piggy Waffles, Lurcher Geeson, and Sweppy Titmarsh!

" LARKS ! "

" It appears that the doings of those terrible creatures, ' The Ball's Pond Banditti,' are to be illustrated and described each week on the front page of Larks ! *Poor Pa was naturally curious to make the acquaintance of these gentlemen, so he invited them all to a winkle tea in the back garden at Mildew Court. He has since observed more than once that he always considered Alexandry and Bill Higgins sultry, but they are lamb-like when compared to the ' Banditti.' However, on Monday next, May 1, the First Number of* Larks ! *will come out, and as it is only a Halfpenny, there's bound to be a big rush for it."—*Tootsie.

Ally Sloper's Half-Holiday 470; 29 April 1893 (W. F. Thomas)

Funny Cuts 37; 21 March 1891 (Alfred Gray)

This Copy of "LARKS!" is a **Railway Accident Life Policy for £50.**

Larks!

FOUNDED AND CONDUCTED BY GILBERT DALZIEL.

Vol. I.—No. 1.] MONDAY, MAY 1, 1893. [HALFPENNY.

THE BALL'S POND BANDITTI

(1.) THE INSPIRATION.

(2.) THE CONSTRUCTION OF THE BANDIT'S CAVE.

(5.) THE OATH OF ALLEGIANCE.

(4.) THE ELECTION OF THE CAPTAIN.

(3.) THE ENROLMENT OF RECRUITS.

(6.) THE COUNCIL OF WAR.

G. Gordon Fraser

(1) "From 'enceforth I hemilates the doin's of the Robber Chiefs of hold!" observed Ticko Scuppins, of the Ball's Pond Clothing Stores. "Sussiety shall tremble at the name of Bloodwing *alias* Brandon Ballyflathers de Bazan!" "Garn!" replied his admiring friends, Gorger Pain, the doctor's youth, and Piggy Waffles, from the grocery establishment, "yer don't mean it!"

(2) But he did, though : and ere long the gloomy walls of the Bandit's Lair frowned upon a patch of waste land near by, frightening the stray cats from their recreation ground.

(3) Next, the reckless Bloodwing enrolled a desperate but chivalrous band of outlaws. Lurcher Geeson, from the butcher's, and Sweppy Titmarsh, from the rag-shop, were the first to join.

(4) Having adopted the name of "The Ball's Pond Banditti," the desperate crew elected a chief to whom fear and pity alike were empty sounds. The name of Bloodwing headed the poll.

(5) Even the bold bloodhound Bocco seemed moved at the darkly impressive scene which ensued as each Bandit swore allegiance to his Captain and comrades. "I, Piggy Waffles, swears on these 'ere gashly relics of morality to execute horders and pleecemen with promptitoode and despatch. Take me dyin' oath ! S'elp me never !"

(6) The band thus organized, dark deliberations took place as to their first raid upon Society, which, however, must, we fear, wait in trembling suspense for the result till next week.

Larks! 1; 1 May 1893 (George Gordon Fraser)

57

1. Well, Jack Sheppard the Younger and Little Boy Pink didn't do very well at Klondyke last time, so they made another start; but this time they laid in some provisions, same as they'd heard was usual. They took pickles and jam.

2. Well, they went by water, according to the usual style of going to Klondyke, and about dinner-time they got hungry. A little ahead they saw a grizzly bear. "We'll dine on this," says Jack, drawing his catapult.

3. It hit the grizzly fair on the chest, but it didn't stop it; and it wasn't a grizzly at all, but a fat man in a fur coat. On, on he came. "They're desprit when roused," sung out Jack. "Watch me lay him out with pickles."

4. They hit him fair, and stopped his shooting career. "On to Klondyke," says Jack Sheppard. "Onst more we're sailing on the bosom of the nasty deep, on to our doom."

5. And they continued to "row," leaving the grizzly unconscious a-dying on his backbone. "Hi, hi!" laughed Jack. "Yonder I see Klondyke," pointing at a house.

6. Next minute they were there. But it wasn't Klondyke. They'd made a mistake; it was the duck-pond at the back of the "Bald-faced Nag," and their relatives were waiting for them.

Big Budget 29; 1 January 1898 (Jack B. Yeats)

Jack Yeats' juvenile delinquents had to be slightly different from the rest, of course. 'Little Boy Pink' sounds innocent enough, but his partner in crime is the junior of no less a highwayman than Jack Sheppard! Their abortive trips to the Klondyke strike a topical touch. Weary Willy and Tired Tim had their juniors, too, and Tom Browne drew them for Cornelius Chips' companion comic, *The Funny Wonder* (p. 59). 'The *Big Budget* Kid' was cast in the mould of an American success, Richard Outcault's 'Yellow Kid', Bowery slang and all. Middle-class delinquents came to comics through Tom Browne, once again riding his favourite hobby (p. 61). Next year he introduced a regular dose of delinquency in the weekly 'Doings at Whackington School' (p. 62). 'Those Terrible Twins' first appeared in the Grand Double Easter Number of *The Halfpenny Comic*. Four weeks later they moved to the front page, ousting the overly adult 'Mr Stanley Deadstone and Co.' (p. 48). Kids may be said to have taken over comics from that fatal date.

No. 284. Vol. XI.   ONE HALFPENNY, EVERY SATURDAY.   JULY 9, 1898.

THE ADVENTURES OF LITTLE WILLY AND TINY TIM.

1. "Willy," murmured Tired Tim, with a smirk, "our sons is 'Chips' of the old block, ain't they?" "Yes, you wicked old jokist, they am," replied Weary Willy; "ain't it WONDER-ful! Well, boys, are you going to join your honourable parients, or would you rather strike out for yourselves?" "Please, pa," crooned Little Willy, "we'd rather strike—wot ho!" "Yes'm," lisped Tiny Tim, "but we'll be on our own; we've had some of your advice, and it hurts."

2. "Tiny," gurgled Little Willy, "now we're on the warpath like the old 'uns, we shall have to buck up, and beat 'em into fits! Hist! likewise skilence! Yonder comes a bloatered haristocrat. We must be on 'im, Timmy!" "We must!" hissed Tim.

3. The unsuspecting youngster came gradually nearer, and then Tiny and Willy made a spring. "T-e-r-emble, ortry one!" they yelled, "for we will 'ave our r-r-revenge! Deliver hup that jam-puff, or take the kinsequences!" "Sha'n't!" said the kid.

4. "Then you must die!" said Tim. "Come hon, Willy; this bold ruffian refuses to obey the commands of the Noble Society of the Secret Himage! Help me to bind him up." "Yow! bor-o-o!" howled the kid. "I'll tell my mother! Booh!"

5. After that they took their helpless victim and bound him to a tree. "Now we must hexecute the fearful dance of death all round him," chortled Willy. "Woo-oo! hi tiddley hi ti! 'ow do yer like that, yer warmint! It's Red Indian, so get yer topknot ready to be scalped!"

6. But a rescue was at hand in the shape of the kid's ma, and so the victim didn't die a dead death after all. "There!" she said (smack! bang!), "'ow do you like that, you murderous villins?" Bang! flosh! cosh! The boys didn't like it at all; but they were too excited to say so. (Then what happened? See next page.)

The Funny Wonder 284; 9 July 1898 (Tom Browne)

1. WE have had a terrible time at this office recently. All the dignity's been knocked out of us all by a kid. One morning when all was quiet, save for the jerky breathing of the Joke ... apparition appeared at the window and biffed our Sub. right on his brain-box. "I say, ... BIG BUDGET?" yelled the terror.

2. "Well, I'm just cooming in; I've sumthin' to tell you," said the apparition. "Pray ... me not. Now I want you all to come and gather round of me. D'year?"

3. ... "Gather round of me," I said, "and there, that office boy's escaping ... right off. Come back, cocky!" and the kid let fly.

4. "There, now, I'm a-goin' ter show yer how ter run dese 'ere Budgets. I've got ... boards outside, and you've each to take one and walk wiv it in the horder I shall men... I'm de 'BIG BUDGET KID,' and don't you forget it.

5. ... Quick march! De last out of de door to be awarded six pellets. Dignity ain't no good ... Now I'm coomin' meself, and de show will start at wunce—prompt—me in front.

6. "Dere! Come on, Editor, and generl staff. Let me menchun dat de fust bloke decamps and spoils de spellin' gits de horizontal firearm. *Left! Right! Left! Right!!* P.S.—I am too ill to say more now about this awful terror. Whatever will he do next?—

Big Budget 91; 1 March 1899 (Frank Wilkinson)

"MISSING."
New Series of Short, Complete Stories of Real Life every week. Mysterious Cases of Missing People. By AN OLD DETECTIVE.

Comic Cuts.

½d.

ONE HUNDRED LAUGHS FOR A HALFPENNY.

No. 344. Vol. XIV.] Registered. ONE HALFPENNY WEEKLY. [December 12, 1896.

THE BOYS AND THE BICYCLE-INFLATORS.

Comic Cuts 344; 12 December 1896 (Tom Browne)

DOINGS AT WHACKINGTON SCHOOL.

BY A SKOLLAR.

THESE PICTURES ARE BY TOM BROWNE, THE POPULAR ARTIST.

1. "Wz did have a fine lark on the 5th. We had a half-holiday, and me an' the other fellars rigged up a guy in the shed. It looked a proper treat.

2. "Well, in the evenin', Snorter, that's our handy man wot drinks like a fish and cleans our boots and makes the corfee (beastly muck, not fit for gentlemen), staggers inter the shed, knocks ovir our guy, and sinks inter the chare hisself. He was in a drunken stupor!

3. "After we had knocked off evenin' prep., and had lited the bonfire, Basher (that's the bully) shouts, 'Four of you kids go to the shed and fetch the guy!'

4. "We went and fetched it, and, by gum! wasn't it heavy! We got it to the bonfire, though——

5. "And pitched it inter the midst of the angry flames.

6. "But the heat woke up old Snorter (for he it was, gentel reder), and he yells and jumps out of the fire and made a horrible fuss. All the littel kids thort it was a ghost or sumfink, and Mrs. Wiggs—our matron. wot looks after our close—phainted in old Whackem's arms. Lor, how we larfed afterwards, you bet!"

Further doings at Whackington School will be described next Thursday. Screamingly funny!

Big Budget 21; 6 November 1897 (Tom Browne)

The Halfpenny Comic 1½

No. 27, VOL. II.   WEEK ENDING SATURDAY, JULY 23, 1898.   ONE HALFPENNY.

THOSE TERRIBLE TWINS! (Sixteenth Adventure. Another ripping Adventure Wednesday next.)

(1) "Deer Reeders, they were cleaning down at home the other day, so we went down to bisness wiv granpa, to keep us out of mischief, ma sed. We took him by the hand so's he wouldn't get lost.

(2) "When we'd got there I ses to Willie, 'wot do we pay these clerks for—for working aint it? And they keep getting down off their stools an goin' out—we'll stop it.' And Willie sed: 'Yes, by gosh—the munkeys!'

(3) "So when they'd orl gone to lunch, we put some sealing-whacks on orl the stools. 'That'll make 'em stick to their work,' sed Willie, 'and stop calling you Tatcho!' And it did too.

(4) "And just becos they couldn't keep popping orf their stools to jaw, they went down to granpa and complaned. They tore them orf at last, but granpa had to pay for 3 noo pairs of trowsis—such a lot of trowser tore off wiv the stools.

(5) "Owever, granpa sed boys would be boys, and he'd half kill us when he got us home. Then he went to lunch, and I sed to Willie 'we must do something to keep ourselves out of mischief,' so we tried to get a little button out of the wall wiv a penknife.

(6) "The button wouldn't come somehow, but the fire brigade did. Granpa had just got back when the firemen pushed their hoses thro' the window and played on him so's no harm should come to him, and he wos quite moistened before they found there wos no fire.

(7) "You'd have thort they'd have bin glad of that, but no, they seemed quite cut-up cos there wos no fire; and granpa sed it wos our fault and we deserved hanging, so he hung us on the hat pegs out of harm's way, and sed he'd half kill us when he got us home.

(8) "So when we got home we put some stuffing in our trowsis so's it wouldn't hurt, but someone must have peached on us, cos granpa sed he didn't wish to be crooel and would only cane us on our hands that time. So it wos orl in vain wos the stuffing.—Yoors trooly, WALLY WANGS."

The Halfpenny Comic 27; 23 July 1898 (Frank Holland)

1. THOSE Twinkleton Twins had collared a monkey from Count Macarooni, the organ-grinder. But why should they go to the mask shop and buy two monkey faces?

2. Now the plot thickens. See, they are dressing the missing link in their togs.

3. And then they just shove it in the kitchen where Mamma is sitting peeling the apples.

4. "Bless us well," says Ma Twinkleton, "wotever's that boy a-doin' of. Theevin' an' upsettin' all them apples, and under me very nose too. I'll larn him.

5. "Come here this instant, you young rampscallion, with yer impidence. We'll see whose master.

6. "Great pippins!! Look at that tail. It ain't one of my twins. It's a monk, that's wot it is.

7. "And there's a couple more of 'em besides. Hellup!! Perlice!! There's a menagerie broke loose."

8. But just then those twins smole rather too loud, and Ma Twinkleton tumbled to the game. "Come this way, you young rascals.

9. "It's lucky we've got that old crate; it'll just do for a cage, and cages is the proper place for wild monks and animiles of the breed." Then those twinlets had to stop there all day instead of going out to play.

Big Budget 138; 3 February 1900

Wilhelm Busch was the founding father of the visual strip cartoon. His contributions to *Fliegende Blätter*, needing no verbal translation, were reprinted around the world: there was a Busch strip in the first issue of *Funny Folks* (7 December 1874). His picture stories for children, the *Münchener Bilderbogen* featuring 'Max und Moritz', were reprinted by Alfred Harmsworth's *Comic Cuts* as 'Tootle and Bootle', and inspired those long-lived American characters by Rudolph Dirks, 'The Katzenjammer Kids'. In turn, Dirks' Hans, Fritz and Mama inspired many British cartoonists to use similar characters (p. 64) and plots (p. 65).

GRANDPA EXHIBITS TREMENDOUS ENERGY FOR HIS AGE.

1. "I FANCY, people and Hooligans, it'll repay you to watch this set out. If you do not recognise that I am monkeying with springs, blame the artist—not the goak. Go hon.

2. "Grandpa is asleep. He does likkle else now, being 74, and daft at that. I am still monkeying with springs. Next.

3. "You can guess how daft the man is when a hat like that doesn't waken him. But then, of course, 74 is a great age for daftiness.

4. "Now, then, we're getting into the thick of it, as the fly said, when it let loose with its hands and fell into the ice-cream. I'm simply goin' to drop these cans. Are you ready, Grandpa? He speaks not. He is ready.

5. "Bang!!!!! And at one mighty rush off his feetses, Grandpa went up to the roof. I thort this act would be wurf watchin'," said the kid.

6. And after the aged one had gone up and down about sixty times, and was getting a ned-ache—Granny rushed in and tried to hold him down.

7. But alars! Grandmother lost by a short neck, and the three-score-year-and-ten man bounced out of the district—bang!—smash through the window into the great world——

8. And floated serenely onwards. "Hi! You carn't come that way," yelled the cop. "'Taint legal." "Ain't it?" bawled the kid. "You don't know Grandpa. When he starts to do a fing he——

9. "DOES IT!! So you see the joke ends happily after all, the cause of the happiness being a corporation cart of lime just passing. And when Grandpa's paid for what splashed out he isn't going to be charged for anything else."

Big Budget 184; 22 December 1900 (Tom Wilkinson)

The Comic Animal

Humans were humans and animals were animals in the Victorian comic. The humanised animal, walking on his hind legs and dressed in neat Etons, would not evolve until the Edwardian age. In an era of order, animals were kept in their place, as pets ('Kinkins the Pug', p. 75) or performers ('Signor McCoy the Circus Hoss', p. 68). The wilder animals turned up in one-off appearances, and the most popular of these was the elephant, thanks to the famous Jumbo (p. 67). All the tramp double-acts adopted unlikely pets once 'Chokee Bill and Area Sneaker' had set the trend with their snake (p. 70). Later came their kangaroo (p. 71), the two bears who augmented the team of Macaroni and Spermaciti to 'The Happy Four' (p. 74), Willie and Tim's Gussy the Flea (p. 99), and Frank Holland's wonderful 'Walter the Croc', who ultimately took over from 'Jimmer Squirm and Spooky Sprat' (pp. 72–3).

WHIT MONDAY.

The week's work done, The Family frisketh.

It ofttimes happens childish sport
Can make us feel like babes again,
And back the happy season's brought
When we were free from grief and pain.

Then ofttimes Wisdom, linked with Age,
On for a bit o' foolin' feels,
And like unto the new-born lamb
In mirthful glee kicks up it's heels.

Ally Sloper's Half-Holiday 56; 23 May 1885 (W. G. Baxter)

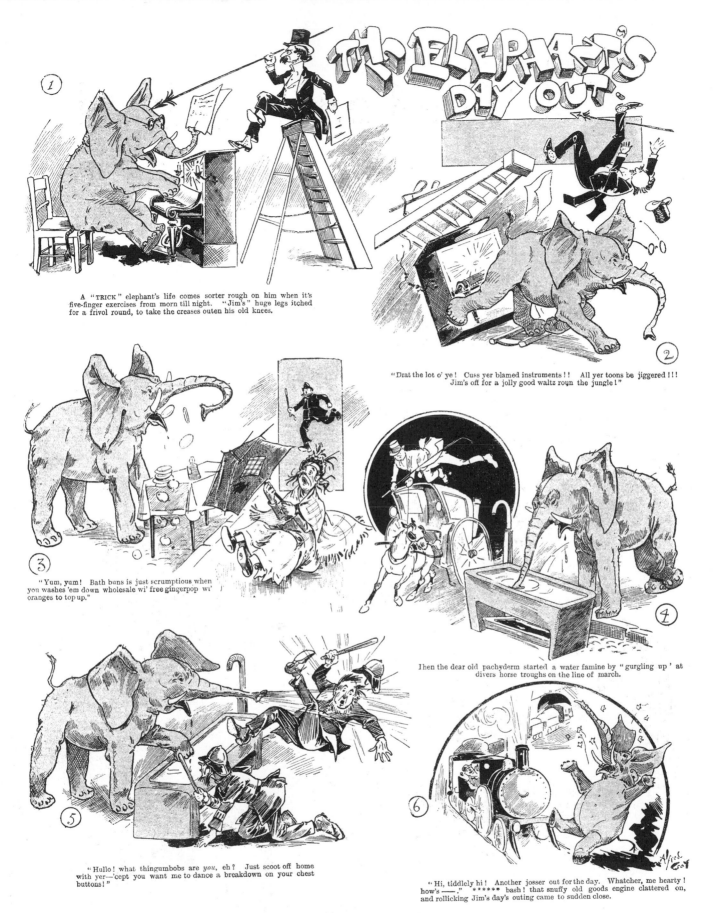

TH' ELEPHANT'S DAY OUT.

1. A "TRICK" elephant's life comes sorter rough on him when it's five-finger exercises from morn till night. "Jim's" huge legs itched for a frivol round, to take the creases outen his old knees.

2. "Drat the lot o' ye! Cuss yer blamed instruments!! All yer toons be jiggered!!! Jim's off for a jolly good waltz roun' the jungle!"

3. "Yum, yum! Bath buns is just scrumptious when you washes 'em down wholesale wi' free gingerpop wi' oranges to top up."

4. Then the dear old pachyderm started a water famine by "gurgling up' at divers horse troughs on the line of march.

5. "Hullo! what thingumbobs are *you*, eh? Just scoot off home with yer—'cept you want me to dance a breakdown on your chest buttons!"

6. "Hi, tiddlely hi! Another josser out for the day. Whatcher, me hearty! how's ——." ****** bash! that snuffy old goods engine clattered on, and rollicking Jim's day's outing came to sudden close.

The World's Comic 75; 6 December 1893 (Alfred Gray)

1. "WE'D got a nice new poster, a startler it was, and startle it did. It startled the inhabitants of Smelt-harbour, I guv yer my word; they'd never seed nuffink like it afore!

2. "Who was going to be the stag, eh? Why ask? Who do yer think could do the part justice but the Signor hisself. At first, when we was a-tying them branching horns on his top-knot, he seemed as mild as butter.

3. "But when we tried to get him to enter the arena —well, there—he gave trouble, not to say no more.

4. "However, at last he was off. The effect was beautiful. The *Smelt Harbour Safety Valve* said: 'The inhabitants of our historic town injoyed last Thursday a treat both intellectual and t'otherwise— well, the audience was satisfied.'

5. "Well, you see, the hunt was to pass *twice* through the arena. That was the trouble. After the first round, it appears, McCoy turned on the hunters, and they had a bit of a dust up outside the tent, and when they came in a second time——

6. "It was the stag as did the huntin'!"

Big Budget 38; 6 March 1898 (Jack B. Yeats)

1. "WE was in the act of entering the town of Spankbourne, in Zomerset" (it's the Circus Man talking), "where there's a boys' school—in fact, it's all boys' school. The Signor had his work cut out not ter s* on 'em, and when he sneaked a cake off one of 'em, Oh my! didn't they squalk and vow revenge.

2. "That very evening at the show, one of them little schollards up and offered McCoy a bun—just when he was a-doing his high jumping act, a-flying over five-barred gates like a hangel (which comes before the clownd and the pig playing football act). Well, the Signor took that bun, and, would yer believe it——

3. "It were loaded—yus, loaded with pepper— such was the revenge of the schollard. Now what did the Signor do?

4. "Well, he went and stood around outside the school, and the clownd, having first fixed a noose handy, put an ole tin can and some string where the schollards couldn't miss 'em. 'Now,' he chuckled, 'a hoss's tail, a tin can, and some string. They can't resist 'em.'

5. "And they couldn't. In course they was at once for tying that tin can on to the hoss's tail. To do it they had to stand inside the noose, you observe. All of a suddent——

6. "McCoy fetched a jump—they was laid

7. "Well, that sagacious quadrupedlar took them schollards through the back parts of the town where the mud was deepest, and then to the——

8. "River. But one of the schollards cut the rope, sudden—so sudden that the Signor sat down on his nose, which annoyed him; but he was rewarded later on.

9. "You see, when those schollards got back to the school-house wet, and dirty, there was ructions. As they lay in a row a-waiting, McCoy looked in. How's that for revenge?

Big Budget 42; 2 April 1898 (Jack B. Yeats)

It was Jack B. Yeats—of course—who created something special out of the animal world. The character he gave to his 'Signor McCoy the Wonderful Circus Hoss' literally bucked off the pages of *Big Budget*, leaving his owner, the Circus Man, standing at the post. The first funny animal hero in comics, McCoy is the undoubted ancestor of such later great haybags as Roy Wilson's 'George the Jolly Gee-Gee' (*Radio Fun*, 1938).

TRADE NOTICE. — NEXT WEEK we shall issue a Monster SEASIDE NUMBER, part Printed in COLOURS. 20 Pages — a Double Number and a half. Orders should be given early.

Comic Cuts.

ONE HUNDRED LAUGHS FOR A HALFPENNY

½ d.

No. 381. Vol. XV.] REGISTERED. ONE HALFPENNY WEEKLY. [AUGUST 28, 1897.

THE ADVENTURES OF CHOKEE BILL AND AREA SNEAKER (continued).

1. "Dear Mr. Editter, — Yer wanter know 'ow we went on wiv that snike we burgled? Lawst you 'eard it wos locked in the celler. Yus! Well, we brung it out, an' tied it to a post in the backyawd ter think erbout it.

2. "Finerly we decided to drownd it. So I puts it in a big back-pocket of a coat an' stawts out.

3. "Orl went well till the snike 'e wriggles out o' me pocket an' pops 'is face out o' the back o' me coat. 'E giv' a gemman wot wos jist behind an orful fright.

4. "Well, I tucks 'im in at the bottom o' me coat, an' 'e worms 'isself art o' the back o' the neck an' stawtled a pawty wot'd ony signed the pledge the night afore.

5. "So I farstens up the collar an' kep' 'old o' the coat-tails ter keep 'im in. Wot does 'e do but bite a 'ole froo the middle o' the back, a-horrifyin' of 2 little grocer-boys in so doin'!

6. "At larst we gits 'im ter the river. I wos just perpoundin' ter Area a few rough ideas on snike-drowndin' —

7. "When that there ungriteful sarpint chucks 'isself out like a spring-coil, and shoots me an' Area 'eadfirst inter the sloshy worter —

8. "Where we stuck! Then 'e sot darn an' larfed. — Yer 'umble, CHOKEE." *24/8/97

Comic Cuts 381; 28 August 1897 (Frank Holland)

TO THE TRADE: A DOUBLE COLOURED SUMMER HOLIDAY NUMBER of "COMIC CUTS" will be published on Saturday, July 30th (Saturday before Bank Holiday). Price 1d.

3d. ONLY. THE HARMSWORTH MAGAZINE.

Comic Cuts.

½d.

ONE HUNDRED LAUGHS FOR A HALFPENNY.

No. 428. Vol. XVII.] REGISTERED.   One Halfpenny Weekly.   [JULY 23, 1898.

THE ADVENTURES OF CHOKEE BILL AND AREA SNEAKER. (The Training of James Enery the Kangaroo.)

1. "DEER MR. EDDITTER,—Ter go back to my animal-trainin' idea. Lawst week I met a gemman wot 'ad travelled wiv a troupe of performin' fleas, an' 'e sed animal-trainin' wos orl done by imitation.

2. "So when we got 'ome we tried it on James Enery the kangaroo. I wanted ter teach 'im a few intellectooal feete—standin' on 'is 'ead an' walkin' on his 'ands, an' sich. So we stawted a-doin' of 'em ourselves fust to eddicate him.

3. "Well, we put our whole souls inter the tawsk. James Enery looked on a bit, an' then seemed ter weary, an' turned round the other way. We waited abart 10 minits for 'im ter turn back agin, but as 'e didn't do so—

4. "We walked rarnd on our dooks an' did dooty on the other side, so's our example wouldn't be lorst on 'im. 'E looked sorter dreamy, I thort, but we stuck to the work of eddicatin' till we wos nearly black in the face—

5. "Till orl at once James Enery started ter snore, and, gittin' up sudden, we farnd 'e wos farst asleep, an' proberly 'ad been orl the time. Werry disheartenin' it wos, but we worn't ter be dornted—

6. "An' whenever we 'ad a little leisure we follered the kangaroo abart the 'ouse, walkin' on our dooks or standin' on our 'eads. At larst 'e seemed to understand, and stawted a-tryin' an' 'e wouldn't give way till 'e could do it.

7. "'E wos at it orl day, an' at night we could 'ear 'im falling erbout the place a tryin' 'ard ter do it. Area yoosed ter wake up terrified. 'E thort it wos burglars, wot 'e's perticklerly nervous erbout.

8. "Finerly, James Enery seemed ter tumble to it, and one mornin' we wos delighted ter come darn an' find 'im standin' on 'is head, like a good 'un; an' as fer walkin' on 'is 'ands, 'e could do it like a bird.   23/7/98

9. "But we wish we'd never started it now, for he's never yoosed his legs since. Now we've started teachin' 'im ter ferget is eddication occasionally, an' sit an' walk as he yoosed to in the parst.—Yer 'umble, CHOKEE."   (Another Set Next Week.)

Comic Cuts 428; 23 July 1898 (Frank Holland)

1. "Deer Mister Edditter,—Take my tip, an' wotever yer do, never sneak a crokkerdial! Yer know that wun as we snook larst week in a sack by mistake? Well, a nice job we've 'ad wiv 'im, I tell yer. Tork erbart a korfdrop. Well, 'e is a korfdrop. 'E seemed 'armless enuff when we got yoosed to 'im, so we let him crorl erbart the place to 'is 'eart's content.

2. "Well, o' coarse, like the rest o' peeple, as soon as we guv 'im a hinch 'e tuk a yawd, an' when me an' Jimmer wos a-sittin' in the drorin'-room, wot does 'e do but cawmly creep orf darnstares as quiet as a mowse—

3. "An' crorl into the bedroom of a gemman wot lives on the fust floor corled Mister Mopper. At it 'appened, Mister Mopper 'ad cum 'ome wearied out wiv' bizness an' beer an' wun fing an' anutther, an' gorn ter bed. "Wot O!" ses Walter (that's the crokkerdial), as 'e shoves 'is snowt in between the kurtens.

4. "Well, o' coarse, that wornt a crime in itself, but 'e didn't stop there. 'E marches 'isself inter the room an' stawts a-toyin wiv' Mister Mopper's trarsis an' fings wot wos 'angin' on a chare. 'Narce pare o' trarsis these,' 'e chuckles to 'isself. 'Wonder 'ow they'd look on my manly form?'

5. "An' wiv that 'e squirms 'isself up 'em, and wuks 'is way up inter the koat an' weskit. Well, 'e wos gittin' erlong werry nicely, thenk yer, when orl of a sudding—

6. "Mrs. Mopper busts in! 'Wot!' she ses, as she seed the toggery wrigglin' erbart on the floor—finkin' it wos 'er 'usband—'Wot! Drunk agane, yoo old repperobate? I'll giv' yer drunk, yoo yooman beer-barrel!'

7. "An' wiv' that she whacks inter Walter for all she wos worth. 'Tek that," she ses, 'yoo walkin' brewerry, an' that an' that!' An', o' coarse, Walter 'ad ter take it. 'Owever, at larst 'e mannidged ter pull 'isself tergether, an' whips rarnd an' faces 'er.

8. "'Woman!' 'e ses, bustin' wiv' rage, ''ow dare yer biff me wiv' a broom like that? Tutch anutther hare of my 'ead if yoo dare, an' I'll screem an' corl a copper!'—Yoors trooly, Spooky the Sprat."

Big Budget 181; 1 December 1900 (Frank Holland)

72

1. "DEER MISTER EDDITTER,—We've 'ad an orful time wiv Walter, the crokker-dial, this pawst week. I reely don't fink we can keep 'im. Corse 'e's a bit o' company for us, an' 'armless enuff in a way, but 'e's so obstropperlus. The other day the milkman left 'is big kan artside the drorin'-room winder.

2. "Well, Walter, as it 'appened, wos just lyin' on the sofer in the drorin'-room, an' 'earin' the kan bein' dumped darn on the pivement, peeps art 'o the winder ter see-wot wos on. Course 'e spots wot it wos in 'arf a jiff, an' a gleam ov greed kums inter his optick.

3. "'Wot, milk? That bewtiful beve-ridge of me child'ood!' 'e ejackerlates, as 'e pushes 'is face inter the kan an' niffs the liquid like a firsty navvy smellin' a pot ov beer arter a 'ard day's work.

4. "'Oh, chase me! I'm on it like a burd!' 'e ses. An' wiv that 'e hownces in like a kart-load o' bricks. An' there wos a sound as though sumbody wos pullin' up worter wiv a fousand 'orse power pump.

5. "'Arf a mo' later back comes the milkman, just as the larst bit o' Walter was diserpeerin' inter the kan. O' corse the man knoo nutthink erbart Walter bein' inside——

6. "An' just as the crock 'ad 'is mouth open, an' the milk wos pourin' darn 'is throte, the milkman dips 'is arm in ter ladle sum moar milk art, an' shoves the kan 'arfway darn Walter's throte.

7. "Natcherally Walter did the same as yer'd ha' done yerself—'e snapped 'is jawrs to, an' bit the pore man brootal. It wos 2 foot long that bite. It started at 'is finger-tipps an' ran rite up parst the elber.

8. "Well, as ennybody knows, there ain't no pleashure in bein' bit by a crok-kerdial. The pore feller neerly yelled the street darn. Bime bye, arfter neerly pullin' the man 'ead-fust inter the kan——

9. "Walter 'avin' got some of 'is own back, let go, an' bobs up sudden like a rokket. When the milkman seed 'im, 'e neerly went orf 'is onion. Just then we 'ears the row an' rushes up.

10. "'Walter!' I yells, 'wot are yoo a-doin' of in that milk-kan? Didn't I ferbid yer to go outside the 'ouse'? Well, as soon as 'e 'eerd my voice 'e flopped darn inter the kan like a shot.

11. "'Cum out, sir, this minnit!' I ses, as we jumps darn onter the pavement. 'E wouldn't cum at fust; 'e sed 'e 'adn't finnished orl the milk. But we wos firm wiv 'im, an' at larst got 'im out.

12. "An', as I karried 'im in, I guv 'im a good torkin' to. 'Walter,' I ses, 'why are yer sich a worry? I do wish yer woodn't be so obstropperlus!'—Yoors trooly, SPOOKY THE SPRAT."

Big Budget 182; 8 December 1900 (Frank Holland)

½D JOKES ½D

JOKES COUPON No. 1.

With which is incorporated "THE JOKER."

No. 1.—Vol. I. THURSDAY, JANUARY 20, 1898. ONE HALFPENNY.

1. " Macaroni," said Spermaciti, " can dat be beer ? " " How can I tell till I've tasted ? " said Mac.

2. They tasted. All four of them tasted several times, and when they were sure it was beer, drank more.

3. " We'll teach 'em," said the Force, disgusted at the loss of so much good liquor.

4. " Dilute it. Mix it with water. Soak 'em through," said the Force.

5. But when those four were freshened up, they were altogether too lively.

6. And when last seen were wearing the helmets and tunics of the defeated Force.

Prize Page, No. 8. Lots of Prizes.

Jokes 1; 20 January 1898 ('M.A.B.')

EXTRACT FROM THE DIARY OF KINKINS THE PUG.

1. "3 p.m.—Round the houses with 'our kid' and little Johnny Fauntleroy. We stop outside a shop where Jeddah, the Derby winner, is on show. Looks as if butter—let alone *Cheddar*—wouldn't melt in his mouth. I wonder what those funny things are it's standing on?

2. "3.30 p.m.—The kid and Johnny are making a Derby winner for themselves. It's Billy — so named because he has whiskers (Billi: ancient goatese word, meaning whiskers). I begin to have a suspicion that Jeddah was a rocking-horse, and that Billy is to be one (beg pardon, rocking-goat).

3. "3.30½ p.m.—Little Johnny Fauntleroy has got the hump badly — not his own, but Billy's. Tommy seems to be enjoying himself; evidently the hump isn't catching. I'm afraid Johnny will fall. But he needn't be so frightened ; I'll catch him.

4. "3.30¾ p.m.—Billy is skating round the garden, so is Johnny. He is holding on frantically to Billy's whiskers. (I forgot to tell you that Billy has whiskers all over him.) I am wondering if it would be well to bite whiskers. It's a good thing Billy keeps his hair on, or where would Johnny be?

5. "3.30⅞ p.m.—Things are getting mixed. I have just remembered an urgent engagement, and the Kinkinses are renowned for their punctuality. Jeddah-Billy has just caught Johnny a back-hander. Tommy is still laughing like a bagpipe.

6. "3.31 p.m.—The laugh has ended in a wrong note. Billy has charged Tommy worse than a magistrate, and without the option of a fine, too. I am not surprised that Jeddah won the Derby now. If it can hop about on those rocker things anything like Billy it will win anything."

Comic Cuts 428; 23 July 1898 (A. H. Clarke)

ROYAL SPORTS IN THE CANNIBAL ISLANDS.

1. The Tinkeroo Island Annual Athletic Meeting took place before the king last week. The meeting opened with a glove contest between Blakasinky and the elephant Jumbo junior.

2. And although it came as a surprise Jumbo junior was knocked out in the third round.

3. The next event was a cycle race. Pongo the monkey took the lead at first.

4. This event, however, was won by a neck by the giraffe.

5. A tug-of-war then took place between niggers and animals.

6. But the rope broke, and the king and his suite got so mixed up that the sports came to an abrupt termination.

Illustrated Chips 361; 31 July 1897 (S. W. Cavenagh)

The animals of an expanding empire inspired a mere handful of miscellaneous strips, but in them may be seen the seeds of such humanised heroes as 'Tiger Tim and the Bruin Boys' of the Edwardian era. Animals are on a par with humans, albeit black ones, in S. W. Cavenagh's 'Royal Sports in the Cannibal Islands', a middle page filler from *Illustrated Chips*.

1. LAST week, in Beebeeland, Mr. Monk, who's getting a dab at cricket, challenged Mr. Sidewhiskers, the tiger, to a match.

2. Then the match started, Mr. Sidewhiskers going in first. "Play," shouted the umpire. "Oh, I shall bowl yer this shot," chortled the monkey.

3. But the first ball caught the tiger in the optic, and he said some very naughty words and began to lose his temper.

4. But the next ball was a fair corker, and bowled him all over the shop. "How's that, umpire?" "Out!" yapped the umpire, and skedaddled, like the wise umpire he was.

5. "Out! is it," growled the tiger. "I'll out yer, you long-tailed, nut-cracking baboon."

6. And ten minutes afterwards the tiger was heard to ejaculate: "Well, people, I fancy I won that match after all. That chap *was* joocy—real joocy, gents."

Big Budget 168; 1 September 1900 (Tom Wilkinson)

Three years later the animals have taken over; there is now no need for a supporting cast of humans. 'Never Challenge a Man Bigger Than Yourself' is still in the filler category, but is set in 'Beebeeland', *Big Budget*'s private comic colony somewhere in the Dark Continent. This idea was lifted from *Comic Cuts*, whose own comic colony was colonised six years earlier, but which was essentially human (p. 112).

The Comic Age

The Victorian Age, unmatched in exploration, invention, and ceremony, was caught in its comics to a surprising degree. Surprising, because to us, today, the comic is an entertainment for juveniles. Both the Queen's Jubilees, 1887 and 1897, were celebrated in the comics (pp. 79 and 82), as was her Birthday (p. 83), her country home (p. 80), and her Memorial to her Consort (p. 81). Victorian personalities turned up in comics: the Prime Minister (p. 84), the leading stage knight (p. 85), and the favourite comedian (p. 86), who was soon given a whole comic paper of his own (p. 87). Tom Browne delighted in topicality and placed his 'Airy Alf and Bouncing Billy' at every national sporting event. Riding the bicycle boom, Alf and Billy also pioneered the latest forms of motorised transport (pp. 96–7).

CHRISTENING OF JUBILEE SLOPER.

" With his well-known fondness for little children, Albert Edward stood Sponsor for Jubilee, who was Christened the other day by the Family Chaplain. On account of Jubilee's inherited dislike for Water, the Chaplain performed his functions in a somewhat flighty manner. Poor Pa got a good sprinkling, and Ma could scarcely hold the Muscular Child. During our inspection of the Silver Mug, given by The Prince, those dreadful Boys behaved outrageously.''—Tootsie.

Ally Sloper's Half-Holiday 148; 26 February 1887 (W. F. Thomas)

GRAND JUBILEE NUMBER.   ONE PENNY.

Ally Sloper's Half Holiday

CONDUCTED BY GILBERT DALZIEL.

Vol. IV.—No. 164.]　　　SATURDAY, JUNE 18, 1887.　　　[ONE PENNY.

ALLY'S JUBILEE TREAT FOR CHILDREN ONLY.

"*Of course Poor Papa is willing to admit that the Daily Telegraph's notion is a good one, but the question that arises in his mind is as t . whether the children might not have been more benefitted had he been consulted first. With this view, the other day, he gave a Jubilee Entertainment on hi own account, and regaled the youngsters on a nutritious and health-giving food, specially prepared by himself and mamma for the occasion, from an old established recipe belonging to his grandmother. Alexandry, too, was on the scene with the celebrated 'Sloper Sally Lunn.'*"—TOOTSIE.

Ally Sloper's Half-Holiday 164; 18 June 1887 (W. F. Thomas)

This Copy of "LARKS!" is a **Railway Accident Life Policy** for £50.

Larks!

FOUNDED AND CONDUCTED BY GILBERT DALZIEL.

Vol. I.—No. 24.]   MONDAY, OCTOBER 9, 1893.   [HALFPENNY.

THE BALL'S POND BANDITTI AT WINDSOR.

(1) A PERILOUS SECRET.

(2) "OUTSIDE, PLEASE!"

(3) THE SUMMONS TO SURRENDER.

(4) VICTORY!

(5) THE ENEMY REPULSED

(6) THE ESCAPE.

(1) "'Ush, Gorger! a word in yer hear," hissed Bloodwing. "You may not 'ave hobserved this wite cockade hin my 'at. 'Tis the hemblum of the Jacobite League, of wich I am now a leader. Study the royal puddigree, but breathe not a word, or my head may roll on the scaffold."

(2) Next day Bloodwing, having hastily enrolled the Ball's Pond Banditti in the Jacobite League, set out for Windsor, to occupy the Royal residence for the Stuart heiress. Proceeding to the Albert Institute, he announced his intention of delivering a lecture on the "Royle 'Ouse of Stooart." A bulky policeman thought differently, and persuaded the young enthusiast to withdraw.

(3) The undaunted Bloodwing next led his trusty band to the Norman Gate of the Round Tower, and demanded the surrender of the Castle in the name of the "Queen Over the Water." No notice was taken of this demonstration, but footsteps were heard approach-ing from the rear, and next moment a servitor appeared, bearing a tray of costly viands.

(4) "Ha!" cried Bloodwing. "He's fetching a chop and a pint of 'four-half' to the Missus I mean the present hoccy-pant of the Throne. Seize 'im! They must be confrustrated!" Instantly the luckless menial was hurled to the ground and robbed of his eatables.

(5) Promptly the guard turned out, and it would have gone ill with the Bandits had not the foremost warrior slipped upon the chop, and, 'ere he could recover himself, been completely prostrated by the dish cover and the pint pot striking his martial visage, hurled by the brawny arm of the Bandit Chief. As it was, the band made good their retreat.

(6) And a few minutes more found them in a borrowed punt, placing the winding Thames between them and pursuit. Poor Bocco had a narrow escape from drowning.—(*See next week.*)

Larks! 24; 9 October 1893 (George Gordon Fraser)

This Copy of "LARKS!" is a **Railway Accident Life Policy** for **£50**.

Larks!

FOUNDED AND CONDUCTED BY GILBERT DALZIEL.

Vol. I.—No. 27.]   MONDAY, OCTOBER 30, 1893.   [HALFPENNY.

THE BALL'S POND BANDITTI AT THE ALBERT MEMORIAL.

(1.) "Gorger, you're right. The Bandit's trade ain't bin ezackly a gold mine of late : but Bloodwing is not yet conkered ! 'Ave the rope-ladder ready at noon, and you shall learn more. Enough ! "

(2.) At the appointed hour the Robber Chief presented himself to his followers in the garb of an artizan. "Fellow Bandits ! " said he, "ere to-morrow's dawn, by the haid of these togs, we shall obtain percesshun of the great gold statoot in the Halbert Memorial, and will proceed to form ourselves into a synagogue of millionaires. Dreckly Piggy Waffles 'as arrove with the bag, we march,"

(3.) Arrived at the Memorial, in temporary concealment behind the pedestal of the allegorical group representing Europe, the Bandits awaited a favourable moment for their Chief to advance with his rope-ladder and ascend to the statue of the late Prince Consort, and remove it as if for repairs, Piggy Waffles holding a bag in readiness for its reception. A hitch, however, occurred. "Cap'," said

Gorger Pain, "you'll 'ave a job to tuck that there great round-backed bloke into this 'ere, and no kid ! "

(4.) Bloodwing's quick brain grasped the solution of the difficulty. Why not remove the statue piecemeal, taking the head as the first instalment ? Prompt to act on an idea, Bloodwing, followed by his lawless Band, after a severe struggle, succeeded in mounting upon the statue. His frantic endeavours to remove the head with a saw were, however, cut short by a yell of alarm from Sweppy Titmarsh, who sighted a body of police advancing below to surround the robbers.

(5.) Their sole chance of safety lay in instant flight. How the ruthless ones escaped uncrippled from that mad, headlong rush it were vain to conjecture.

(6.) Bloodwing, the last to fly, only escaped capture by a lucky cast of the rope-ladder, which caused his nearest pursuer to seat himself in a careless attitude on the pavement,—(See next week.)

Larks! 27; 30 October 1893 (George Gordon Fraser)

THREE PAPERS FOR A PENNY!

The Big Budget. 1d

First Number of a New Paper.

| VOL. I. No. 1. | WEEK ENDING SATURDAY, JUNE 19, 1897. | PRICE 1D. |

THE ADVENTURES AND MISADVENTURES OF AIRY ALF AND BOUNCING BILLY.—AT THE JUBILEE PROCESSION.

1. Airy Alf and Bouncing Billy arrived at Charing Cross in full court uniform to see the Jubilee procession. There was a frightful crush, and they got severely damaged.

2. "Let's get out o' this," said Airy Alf. "Right ye are," says Bouncing Billy; "we'll sprint up to St. Paul's and see the whole show."

3. "Put it on, ole man," shrieked Airy Alf. "The guards are after us with drawn swords."

4. They might have got away all right, had not a couple of tykes got in the way and sent them headlong into a £10 plate glass window.

5. The swells got riled at A. A. and B. B.'s sudden entry and began to give them what for. The crowd shouted with laughter, and even forgot to look at the show.

6. But a couple of stalwart bobbies soon stopped the game, and Airy Alf and Bouncing Billy spent the remainder of the day in quod, and saw no procession after all.

Big Budget 1; 19 June 1897 (Tom Browne)

LONG LIVE THE QUEEN

THE Big Budget 1d

VOL. VI. No. 154.　　WEEK ENDING SATURDAY, MAY 26, 1900.　　PRICE ONE PENNY.

AIRY ALF AND BOUNCING BILLY SPOOF THE BARMY ASYLUM PEOPLE.

1. "BROKE agin," murmured a voice—it was that of Airy Alf. "As broke as Kruger's smeller," moaned another voice, which belonged to the one and only Bouncing Billy. "Wot's ter be done?" groaned Alf. "Oo's ter be done, yoo mean," purred Billy. "Har, har! a nidear! Look at that notis." And the plot was plotted there and then.

2. "'Ow do I go now?" squeaked Billy. "Jist a litt'e more on that pimple on yer boko," prattled Alf, "and you'll lo k a bigger ijiot than nacher made yer." "None o' yer cheek," growled Billy, "or I chucks the job." And, for a moment, it looked like another row between the bounders, but Alf rammed the paint brush in Billy's mouth, and crooned, "I was only chaffing yer, pudding hed. Come on. Let's git yer chains on."

3. Of course you see the game now, dear reader. We thought you would. Ah, what will they be up to next, as you say? To resume. "Bless yer, mum," gurgled Alf, to an old girl standing by, "there ain't no occasion ter be alarmed. I've gottim hunder pu'fect control. Wot made 'im mad, mum? 'E was carst hon a dessert island wiv nuffink but Kronic Cuts ter read for six months. 'Nuff ter make anyone barmy, ain't it?"

4. "Thankee, sir," chortled Alf, "I capehered 'im jest by the duck pond in Hyde Park, arfter a desprit struggle ov 4 days and an arf. Keep 'im safe, sir. 'E's werry wiolent, and if he ekscapes agin jist wire fer me, care hof the Dook of Barking, 13, Marlborough Palace."

5. Five minutes afterwards, of course, the terrible fraud was discovered, and a figger shot out of the barmy asylum like a penny rocket. "It's verry forchenate," murmured Billy, "that I took the precorshun of padding me pants wiv ten pounds of sofa stuffing, 'cos these 'ere asylum chaps don't 'arf know 'ow to use those number seventeen trilbies of theirs. Nar fer a nice sorft bit of pavement to fall on and I'm orl rite."

6. Then, after dividing the spoil, the two bounders rigged themselves out and went off to the Exhibition. "Flossie," murmured Billy, to the pretty waitress, "bring hus another bottle of the same as before. We've jist bin ter see our ole pal, Cecil Rhodes, and 'e's given hus a couple o' pounds ov diamonds each fer showin' French 'ow ter relieve Kimberley."

Big Budget 154; 26 May 1900 (Ralph Hodgson)

MAY I TEMPT YOU WITH A FIVE-POUND NOTE?

See Page 5,
Comrades' Budget.

The Big Budget. 1d

The Cash Department is
Page 5, Comrades' Budget.

VOL. II. No. 30.　　　WEEK ENDING SATURDAY, JAN. 8, 1898.　　　PRICE 1D.

AIRY ALF AND BOUNCING BILLY INTERVIEW MR. J. CHAMBERLAIN, M.P.

1. A.A.: "Aw, aw—I, aw, say, Chief Hinspector, we want to see our pal, Joey Chamberlain."

2. Joseph appears. They interview him. "Wot a hintelectual profile, Alf!"

3. "Nice chap, 'aint he, Billy?" "Yus; I'm a-going inside the 'ouse ter sit next to 'im."

4. "Please, Mr. Speaker, will yer show hus where Joe sits?"

5. But in two jiffs the Sergeant-at-Arms removed them to the door."

6. Where they encountered the boot of the policeman, and this landed them outside into the hard, cold world. "M.P.'s ain't got no decent breedin', not at all, they ain't."

Big Budget 30; 8 January 1898 (Tom Browne)

DAN LENO'S COMIC JOURNAL, ½ᵈ. NOW ON SALE.

The Big Budget. 1ᵈ

Last week of McCoy £25 Competition.

You are still in time to enter.

VOL. II. No 37.   WEEK ENDING SATURDAY, FEB. 26, 1898.   PRICE 1D.

AIRY ALF AND BOUNCING BILLY INTERVIEW ✶ SIR HENRY IRVING.

Alf and Billy looked just scrumptious when they went to interview Sir Henry Irving at the Lyceum. "Princes at the very least," murmured the attendants. "This way to the Royal box, yer Grace."

2. Then Sir Henry came upon the scene, and they were introduced. "Jest smile a tragedy snore, old man," chortled Alf, the artist. "Kindly tell me wot 'air oil yer great-grandmother used," murmured Billy, the interviewer.

Later Miss Ellen Terry appeared. "Crumbs," gurgled Alf, "be calm thou little fluttering Billy sighed a sigh. "Oh that we two were maying," he lisped.

4. "Billy," said Alf, as they departed with jaunty air and very big smiles (the jaunty air is in Alf's portfolio). "Billy, interviewin' is our forte! We never made a bloomin' slip—" But he spoke too soon.

A big trap door in the stage had been let open. "Jerusalem!" moaned the interviewer did the vanishing demon trick, "there's going to be a sudden stop soon!" and they

6. In the cold and clammy dead of night they wheeled the fragments of the pair home to happy Camberwell. "Cats' meat!" yelled the crowd. "Alf," faltered Billy, "this is the larst straw." Anyway, it gave them the hump.

Big Budget 37; 26 February 1898 (Tom Browne)

85

This is the **PICTURE RIDDLE** paper. £5 a week.

The Big Budget. 1d

You are just in time to begin our new serial.

VOL. II. No 33.　　WEEK ENDING SATURDAY, JAN. 29, 1898.　　PRICE 1D

AIRY ALF AND BOUNCING BILLY INTERVIEW DAN LENO.

1. A. A. and B. B. are commissioned to interview Dan Leno at Drury Lane panto-
mime. Having hired some dress togs, they set out. The power of the press, and half-
a-crown, enables them to pass through the stage door.

2. The first things they see are a lot of supers in awful masks. "Help! help!" yells
Alf. "Spare me! O spare me!" groans Billy; "I will never touch anyfink stronger
than soda and milk again."

3. Suddenly Dan Leno and Herbert Campbell appear upon the scene. "'Alf! prince
of panto!" says Billy. "Don't mind if I do," answers Daniel, "in a tankard, please."

4. All went well until the end of the first act. A. A. and B. B. are lost in admiration of the beautiful chorus girls. A scene-shifter bears down on them with a piece
of scenery. The illustrious pair are hurled forward on to the stage——

5. Just in time to get caught by the curtain as it goes up on the transformation scene.
The audience think a parachute act is about to begin, and cheer as A. A. and B. B. are
taken higher and higher. They alight in the wings and sneak round the back way.

6. A. A. and B. B. escape with their lives. The actors hoot them as they hurry out.
"Alf," mutters Billy, "if I don't see yer agin—hullo! Come and restore your shattered
nerves at the Purple Periwinkle."

Big Budget 33; 29 January 1898 (Tom Browne)

£20. £20. £20. SPLENDID NEW COMPETITION. £20. £20. £20.

DAN LENO'S COMIC JOURNAL ½

No. 43. VOL. II.
WEEK ENDING
December 17, 1898

"ONE TOUCH OF LENO MAKES THE WHOLE WORLD GRIN."

EVERY TUESDAY.

DANIEL ON THE BUST.

1. "DEER REEDERS.—The boss a got r on the brane. On Friday, **Lord Debroke** an I **Gussie Smiffsmaffe** korled round 2 see wever they kood get a drink on the cheep. Lord Debroke ad growed a be-yo-tiful mustash, and Par, so ad sum mo'elling klay on the tabel, sed: 'Ho! Wot luvli wiskers! Let me make a portrait bust of yew, melord.'

2. "'Righto, deah be-hoy,' gurg'ed his ludship. Yew see, deer reeders, e's ded knuts on anneyfing 2 B got on the cheep. Then the ole man started slamming the klay about with a puttey-gnife. 'Just look pleasant, melord,' ered. 'My, ain't them wiskers just orlrite!' Me and ower nig did s m grinning, yew bet.

3. "But we grinned a bit moar wen the gloryus werk of art was finished. 'Ain't it trew 2 natcher, sum?' sniggered the ole man, proudli. 'Just look at the kurl of them wisker'. Wy, it's realer than life!' But is ludship didn't seem p'ezs'd. 'Yew miserabel ole fr'rd,' e yelled, 'is that serposed 2 B me? I'll ave the lor on yew.'

4. "And then **Gussie Smiffsmaffe** mermered: 'Say, Debroke, wy shoo n't me and yew, deer f'ler, maik a life-sized statchew of Dan Leno, bai Jove?' It seems they fort it a good ideer, fer they started slamming klay at the boss just like e was an Arnt Sally. There must ave be n sum glew in that klay, fer——

5. "Every bit that it im stuck like wax. My ribs is soar stil with laffing. An I wen they a l konverted the o e man in2 a larster statchew, the parc of 'em wished im a Merri Christmuss and hooked it. Deer reeders, ave yew ever laffed til orl the battins kame orf yewr wastekote? That's wot me and ower nig di lars Fri'ay. It was orlrite.

6. "That klay was so ea y and sticki, the boss koodn't move at orl, xs pt 2 wink. E never sed a ord owing 2 the klay beeing p'arstered ver is torlki g-mashe n. I shoold kno like 2 rite down ot e fort, Bkors Leno is k ot prin ed in b ew ink now. Wen Mar kame bak from shopp ng she a l ineti-2 phits, and the dor g is st l unwel. With lv, DANNY, JUNE."

All Rivals Outrivalled.

Dan Leno's Comic Journal 43; 17 December 1898 (Tom Browne)

THREE PAPERS FOR A PENNY!

The Big Budget. 1d

This is the greatest Triple Alliance the World has ever seen.

VOL. I. No. 5.　　　WEEK ENDING SATURDAY, JULY 17, 1897.　　　PRICE 1D.

THE ADVENTURES AND MISADVENTURES OF AIRY ALF AND BOUNCING BILLY AT HENLEY.

1. Airy Alf and Bouncing Billy went to the Henley Regatta on a patent water cycle, the invention of Airy Alf. "Come back!" shouted the people, "you'll spoil the race!" "Norrabit," shouted Bouncing Billy. "We're all serene, old cockey," gurgled Alf.

2. But in trying to get through one of the lock gates they got too near, and were half drowned. "Silly cuckoo," warbled Alf, as half a ton of cold water streamed down his back. "Lemme get home," spluttered Billy.

3. After considerable labour they arrived at Henley, and got on the course. "Come off!" roared everybody. But they couldn't move. Something had gone wrong with the steering apparatus. "All is lost," sighed Alf, "tell mother I died game." "Rats!" retorted Billy, "why didn't you invent something safe?"

4. On came the racing crews. Whish! smash!!! bang!!! and Airy Alf and Billy the bouncing one were floundering in the damp and chilly Thames.

5. The river police came along armed with boathooks and poles, and the two champions were fished out wet and worried.

6. The invention was bust and useless. Without a murmur A.A. and B.B. allowed themselves to be carted back to town on a donkey barrer, with the broken cycle on top of them, and the jeers of a heartless mob ringing in their ears.

Big Budget 5; 17 July 1897 (Tom Browne)

McCOY COMPETITION. (£25 IN PRIZES.)

The Big Budget. 1d

DID YOU GET "LOVE STORIES," ½d.
YESTERDAY? THE DAINTY LITTLE PAPER.

VOL. II. No. 35.   WEEK ENDING SATURDAY, FEB. 12, 1898.   PRICE 1D.

AIRY ALF AND BOUNCING BILLY INTERVIEW THE ASTON VILLA FOOTBALL TEAM.

1. A. A. and B. B. are commissioned to interview the captain of the Aston Villa Football Team. They had to go by excursion train. "Sit tight," yell the other occupants of the carriage. "We'll get yer aht wiv a sardine-opener, wen we git there."

2. Arrived at the ground, they make straight for the dressing-room. But the bobby outside took them for "dud-pinchers," and ordered them off.

3. As Devey came out they nobbled him. "Wot 'o, Devey!" they cry; "'arf a mo'! We've got to interview you. 'Ow —— ?" But Devey gave them the go-by.

4. "We shall 'ave to wait till 'e's done chivvying that ball," said Alf. But Billy had got the hump, and said nothing.

5. At last the illustrious pair got sick of doing nothing, and ventured on to the field of play to interview Devey while playing. Alf opened his mouth, and one of the players had a pot shot at it. And not such a bad shot either.

6. And then the crowd had their whack. And after they had wiped their boots on A. A. and B. B., and played tunes on them with their walking-sticks, the happy pair remembered an important engagement at home. Alf is advertising for a head-ache cure.

Big Budget 35; 12 February 1898 (Tom Browne)

89

The Big Budget. 1d

£25 FOR A FEW MOMENTS' WORK. SEE PAGE 82.

Vol. III. No. 58.   WEEK ENDING SATURDAY, JULY 23, 1898.   PRICE 1D.

AIRY ALF AND BOUNCING BILLY PLAY TENNIS.

1. "Twenty-five quid!" gasped Billy, "and jest fer pattin' a ball abaart. I'm goin' in fer that if I 'ave ter porn me dress-suit." Alfy gurgled a gurgle. "Wot a sorft snap, eh? Let's enter. Lead hon!"

2. They didn't know much about the game, and when they were drawn to play each other in the first round the spectators giggled. "Now fer a swipe round!" yelled Alf. "Play hup, and keep a straight bat."

3. Booch! Billy stopped it with his eye. When he'd finished seeing fireworks, he murmured: "Be gum, if I thort yer'd done that a-purpose, I'd come round and slay yer. Chuck bowlin' yorkers, fathead. I've got no pads on."

4. Then it was Willyum's turn, and it would have been a boundary except for Alfie's waistcoat. "'Ow's that humpire?" roared Billy. "'Aint that leg before wicket?" The umpire smiled. "Love all!" he hollered.

5. Sad to say there was no love about it. If you can see any in this picture we'll settle an income on you for life and more. "I'll give yer takin' me fer Aunt Sally!" hissed Alf. "Yer'll be like a mashed tater when I've done," snarled Billy. Biff! biff!

6. "I wouldn't 'ave minded the five bob entrance fee so much," mused Billy, as they were borne from the stricken field, "It's the doctor's bill I'm thinking of." And Alf hisped: "Rock me ter sleep, muvver; rock me ter sleep; the day has been weary and long." (No flowers.)

Big Budget 58; 23 July 1898 (Tom Browne)

A Stamp Album for 10 coupons. See inside for result of first month's presents.

The Big Budget. 1d

NEW SERIAL JUST STARTED.

Vol. V. No. 106. WEEK ENDING SATURDAY, JUNE 24, 1899. PRICE 1D.

AIRY ALF AND BOUNCING BILLY AS GRACE AND RANJITSINHJI.

1. "Wot toe," murmured Billy, "if me old pals Grace hand Ranji ain't in fer a bit of fat." But Alf was thinking big thinks. What about? Well, just look at picture No. 2.

2. Here they are, togged up as Grace and Ranji, wending their way from the railway station. "Hain't the people fond of hus, Billy?" sniggered Alf. "So they ort to be," warbled Billy. "Luk wot we've done fer cricket."

3. "In presenting these so'id gold cups to the world's greatest cricketers," said the Mayor of Muggleton, "it is with feelings"——"Shut-hup, chin moosic," cooed Grace—we mean Billy—"hand over the articles, quick."

4. "Stars and stickjaw," howled Alfred Ranji. "We're a kuppel of cold corpses. There's Gra e and Ranji." And Billy moaned: "Jest has we were a-goin' orf to see wot we could get on the go'ding goblets too."

5. And it was Grace and Ranji, too—turned up in the nick of time. "Well, I never!" said old W. G., "if it ain't the BIG BUDGET boys. We are pleased to see 'em, ain't we, Ranji?" And the pals howle'l: "Leggowi'lyer. Wehivn'tdunnuflink."

6. "Billy," sobbed Alf, after the two B.B. boys had been kicked outside. "Cricket's a reglar frord." And Billy moaned: "You're right. You won't cop me playing for Hingland ag'in. And Grace and Ranji cooed out: "Good-bye. Mind the step, and don't forget to call again."

Big Budget 106; 24 June 1899 (Ralph Hodgson)

THE BOAT RACE No 1

Big Budget 1d

VOL. VI. No. 146.   WEEK ENDING SATURDAY, MARCH 31, 1900.   PRICE ONE PENNY.

AIRY ALF AND BOUNCING BILLY GET INTO WOE AND TROUBLE AT THE BOAT-RACE.

1. THE two cheeky bounders were swaggering along by the training quarters of the Oxford crew. "They all think I'm the Hoxford stroke," sniggered Alf. "Think you're Charley Peace," prattled Billy. "It's me they've got their peepers on. They know by me figger that I'm a regular aflete."

2. "Pip, pip," tootled the pair. "Coming our way, duckies. We're just goin for a quiet walk afore the race. Come and 'ave a plateful of winkles round the corner just to wish us luck." And the two 'Varsity fellows murmured : "Sorry to interrupt you chaps with our girls but you really must——"

3. Biff—biff—"Go"—biff—whack—"before we use force"—thump. "Yow," wheezed Alf, "me perripolitus is broken in free places." "Whoo," howled Billy, "wot d'yer mean by takin liberties with us afore we've bin introduced."

4. It so happened that the *Battersea Belle* with a cargo of sticky coal tar happened to be passing by, and the B.B. boys just dropped in. "Ugh," murmured Alf. "I only 'ad breakfast arf an hour ago. I don't want nothink more to eat." "Don't splash me," chortled Billy. "Keep on your own side."

5. They got the hoisting tackle in motion and the noble heroes were pulled forth. "Whaggerorl laffinat," spluttered Alf as the crowd smiled somewhat. "Aincher seen a gendleman afore?" And a muffled voice from beneath the tar murmured : "Whadswon, Ogsford or Gambridge? I've godabob on Ogsford."

6. "Billy," moaned Alf, after they'd spat out some of the tar, "it'll take gallons of beer to git the taste of this 'ere stuff out of me mouth." "Same here," gurgled Billy. "Wot unfeelin cruel brutes them University-fellers is. This 'ere Boat Race is a frord. It ort to be done away with," wheezed Alf.

Big Budget 146; 31 March 1900 (Ralph Hodgson)

BIG PENSIONS FOR READERS. £1, 10s., 5s., 2s. 6d. A WEEK FOR SIX MONTHS.

The Big Budget. 1ᵈ

THE LARGEST LIST OF VALUABLE PRIZES EVER OFFERED TO READERS, SEE NEXT PAGE.

VOL. I. No. 17.　　　WEEK ENDING SATURDAY, OCT. 9, 1897.　　　PRICE 1D.

AIRY ALF AND BOUNCING BILLY AT THE EXHIBITION.

1. "Wot abaart goin' ter the hexibishun, Alf?" "It'll do me praad, Billy; we'll be 'avin' a toff time there."

2. First thing was, Billy couldn't get through the turnstiles; they had to lift him over. After a bump or two they got him on the other side. They left their jiggers at the door.

3. After looking around a bit, they order some refreshment. "Hello, ducky, 'ow goes it?" "There you are, you giddy kipper," &c., &c. But that girl didn't like it, and——

4. Her young man, who was one of the attendants and very big, came up and hustled them a bit.

5. After that he gently dropped them both into the ornamental lake.

6. When they crawled out the police came and ordered them off the ground for creating a disturbance. "This show is no blooming clarse, is it, Billy?" "Norrahit."

Big Budget 17; 9 October 1897 (Tom Browne)

Funny Cuts 45; 16 May 1891 (Alfred Gray)

1. 'Twas dark, and Tintogs, being weary, lay down to rest under a tree, while Sancho Panza, his pal, sat far into the night cooking and eating a sparrow which he had captured with the aid of a pinch of salt cleverly placed upon its tail. Truly, Tintogs' tin costume made a first-class stove.

2. As Tintogs slept, he dreamed a dream, and in it he saw himself and Sancho, his faithful servant and bottlewasher, mounted upon a fearsome machine. He saw himself conquering fearful foes and rescuing many maidens.

3. When he awoke he straightway set himself to fashion the fearsome thing of his dream. Tintogs surveyed the result of his labour with pride, Sancho with wonder. "Great lollipops! What have the idiots been making?" muttered the old mare, as she poked her handsome al in at the window.

4. And when those bold inventors rode away together on their tandem, the deserted cattle stared in amazement. "What ho, Polly! look here!" gasped the cat's-meat-man's hope. "They've been and gone and chucked us out of work." "Give us the sack? Not much!" exclaimed the indignant moke. "Let's follow them."

5. Later in the day the intrepid cyclists stop at a wayside inn, and wetteth their whistles. coming out they witnessed the above scene. The mare and the moke were taking their enge upon their defenceless enemy.

6. As they rode along later, Tintogs on his steed, Sancho on Pollywog, the moke, Tintogs did swear an oath of oaths. "By yonder setting sun! I swear this day, that from this hour, until I lay me down to die, my only seat shall be my faithful cat's-meat, and if she die I will corpse myself!" And Sancho muttered: "Ditto, I swear!" (Another adventure next Tuesday)

Comic Cuts 443; 5 November 1898 (Tom Browne)

THREE BRIGHT AND CHEERFUL PAPERS FOR A PENNY.

The Big Budget. 1ᵈ

£1 A WEEK FOR SIX MONTHS AS POCKET MONEY (SEE P. 2).

VOL. I. No. 16.   WEEK ENDING SATURDAY, OCT. 2, 1897.   PRICE 1ᴅ.

AIRY ALF AND BOUNCING BILLY AND THE MOTOR-CYCLE.

1. "I wonder what it's like ter ride one of them things, Billy?" "Dunno. Let's 'ave a little go while the old cove's away."

2. "Whoa! you've put the wrong lever on yer fat-headed hidiot. Stop 'er! whoa!" But that motor-cycle had got the bit between her teeth, as it were ——

3. And pranced along in grand style. A Ladies' Boarding School hove in sight ——

4. So they went right bang through the French window, into the schoolroom and out the other side. On, on they went ——

5. Smack through Farmer Turmut's farmyard.

6. Then, after plugging over several ploughed fields, they finished up their wild career by banging through a stone wall into a dirty, muddy, slimy pond, where the blessed motor bust up. A. A. and B. B. will be out of prison next week.

Big Budget 16; 2 October 1897 (Tom Browne)

THREE PAPERS FOR A PENNY!

The Big Budget. 1d

ur First Number made
500,000 people laugh.

VOL. I. No. 3. WEEK ENDING SATURDAY, JULY 3, 1897. PRICE 1D.

THE ADVENTURES AND MISADVENTURES OF AIRY ALF AND BOUNCING BILLY.

1. Airy Alf knew a man who had a motor-car and wished to try it against a cycle to Brighton **I'll** take him on," says Bouncing Billy.

2. And whilst the crafty and Airy Alf occupied the man's attention by talking, the wicked and Bouncing Billy went and bored a hole in the petroleum tank of the motor.

3. They started all right. The motor-man was cock sure of winning. But that's because he couldn't his oil running out at the back.

4. Half way down the petroleum gave out. The motor stopped with a diabolical hiss. And the Airy A. and the Bouncing B. rode merrily on chortling with wicked glee.

5. And when the motor-man got off and found that his tank leaked, and that there was no oil to be until he reached Brighton, he just said a few words that are prohibited in Sunday schools and danced dance of madness and despair.

6. There was nothing for it but to get a horse and take the *horseless* carriage along to Brighton, where the motor man found Airy Alf and Bouncing Billy drinking at his expense. "Alf a mo—tor," chuckled B. B.

Big Budget 3; 3 July 1897 (Tom Browne)

1. "Look 'ere," murmured Phil, as he spotted the superannuated 'tater-can, "wot say f we start a motor-car?"

2. The menagerie said it was a great idea, and then Phil started fixing up. "Now, if you both go underneath," he said, "and I tie you up, you can set the machine going."

3. Then he took the car into the town. "Walk hup, gents!" he howled; "have a ride in the splendidest motor-car ever built." And the gents were on it.

4. Off went the car; and for a while all went well. Then, in the thickest part of the town, Billy and Bones thought it time to show how fast they could move.

5. And kept on doing so. "Gr-r-r-ip!" gurgled the passengers. "Let's make our wills before we die!" And the crowd smelt danger and vamoosed.

6. But farther on there was a bend in the road that went down-hill, and—whizz! cosh! wallop! Down went the motor into a party of picnickers, who didn't seem to like it somehow.

7. And now Phil is wondering whether Billy and Bones will ever get over it.

The Funny Wonder 284; 9 July 1898

OUR GRAND NEW STORY SEE PAGE 3

ILLUSTRATED CHIPS

1½ᴅ

No. 498. Vol. XX. (New Series.) [Entered at Stationers' Hall.] PRICE ONE HALFPENNY. [Transmission Abroad at Book Rates.] March 17, 1900.

WEARY WILLY, TIRED TIM, AND GUSSY OUT ON THE GIDDYFLITS.
The Reason of Our Latest Trouble With France.

1. It was the mumpy month of March, dear reader; and while people were sneezing around and mopping their noses with their handkerchiefs, Willy, Tim, and Gussy started off to see how the Man in the Moon was off for firewood. "Goodbye, all!" they twittered. "We are going to enjoy ourselves, you see. Sorry you can't join in the fun."

2. But they hadn't gone far before a double-barrelled, anti-sideslip, check-action gust of runaway wind bobbed up from nowhere. "Hellup!" cried Tim; "me fairy form is about to bump!" "Nunno!" yelled Willy, "not on me! Shift your little barrel in another direction, or me cramponium is broke for ever! Yow! Ho-oh!"

3. Squish! Tim had "bumped," but it was on to the top of Willy's balloon. "Save me! oh—save me!" he yelled. "Don't let yer ole pal fall so low in the world. I'm so miserable. Bo-oh!" "Gerrout!" snarled Willy. "You go and be miserable on your own contraption. I've got troubles enough of me own!"

4. Just then along came another big puff, and blew the whole bilin' of 'em overboard. "Whither away, friend William?" quoth Tim. "And what's the hurry?" "Can't stop—can't stop!" piped Willy. "I've been ordered south all of a sudden!" "Wot price me?" shrieked Gussy. "Don't forget that I'm in the pictures, and want people to look at me as well as you!"

5. Now it happened that a French warship was cruising about catching winkles, and Willy and Tim made a bee-line for it. "Ship ahoy!" howled Willy as he dived down the smoke-hole. "Come aboard, sir!" chirped Tim, "although I didn't want to. Now then, me merry men, out with the jolly-boat and hoist me slacks off this gaspipe, or I'll get singed! Yoh-ho!"   17/3/00

6. "Vot is de meaning of dis intrusion—eh!" demanded the French captain when the ragamuffians were brought before him. "What 'trooshun?" asked Willy. "Don't you 'come it' with us, Mister Froggie, or you'll get a biff in the duff-box. My little chum here is Lord Wolseley's best pal, and he hates to be insulted. "Corkspettoboosh!" yelled the captain. And then the faithful pair knew that trouble was in store.

(If you miss Willy and Tim's adventures in next Thursday's CHIPS, ½d., you'll be miserable for ever afterwards.)

Illustrated Chips 498; 17 March 1900

THE GRAND XMAS DOUBLE NUMBER of the WONDER Comes out on SATURDAY GET IT.

ILLUSTRATED CHIPS 1D ½

No. 430. Vol. XVII. (New Series.) [Entered at Stationers' Hall] PRICE ONE HALFPENNY. [Transmission Abroad at Book Rates] November 26, 1898.

WEARY WILLY AND TIRED TIM TAKE AN AERIAL TRIP.

1. Last week the two beauties heard that the marvellonious Professor Balmy had invented another flying-machine, and they thought they real'y ought to try it. You see them above on the try. "Careful, Willy," chortled Tim; "I believe I heard a policeman's beat. Since that circus biz me nerves is all untied." "Awright, old onion chiv," said Willy.

2. But they got the new machine out all right, and soon got it started. "Whey ho!" gurgled Willy, "'ere we go; orf to visit aunty. Ta-ta, Mr. Perliceman! 'Member us to the Sirdar." "Well I'm blowed!" said the slop, "if that don't beat Christmas!"

3. "Ho, Willy!" murmured Tim, "ain't it lovely to fly like a bluebottle? Look hup! Mind you don't cannon that cloud. You might hurt him." "Timerthy," growled Willy, "'old yer fat-'eaded row. You'll go and bust the works if you make any more of them terrible jokes."

4. And Willy got so confused like that he pulled the wrong lever, and down they went like a thunderbolt with the horrors. "Oh, Willy," cheeped Tim, "don't let your poor little pal fall, will yer? It's so juicy down there." "Shuttup!" replied the anxious Willy.

5. At last one of the sails got caught in a mountain, and they both got chucked. "Goo'bye, Willy," tootled Tim. "Tell your mother I died thinking o' me. Oo-o-o-o!" "Timerthy, send a eagle up to the rescue," roared Willy.

6. But they both fell on something soft, and so came out topside-up in the finish. They found they were on the Havyerliver Islands, and the natives, being struck by their singular beauty, elected them their rulers on the spot. "William," yapped Tim, "this strikes me as being a bit of yum. 'Ow does yer crown fit?" "Awright," said Willy. "Serlave Aircut, fetch hus a sossidge-roll!"

[They'll be back in time for next week's number, you see if they're not.]

Illustrated Chips 430; 26 November 1898 (Tom Browne)

1. OLD GREENGAGE has been getting a bit skittish lately. The other night he went to a music-hall to see the biograph. "Ah've never sin 'em befower," said he, to a young man on his left, "so ah doan know whether ta expect singers, moosicians, or what." Then the lights were lowered. "Great Pip! there be a train coming s right for us."

2. Then old Greengage sprang up and waved his red cotton handkerchief. "Hi! danger on the line! Can ye no see the red flag? Hi! hi!" But still the express came on. Really, of course, it was just the biograph picture on the screen, but the old josser hadn't seen a biograph before.

3. "Waal, the boss-eyed gawker's running it, doan take any notice, all make a rush for it." Then the old chap howled: "A'm orf afore I get runned over." And he did run, as you can see in the picture. And the people said things about old Greengage that weren't at all nice.

4. "Ah!" the josser said pantingly, when he got outside the theatre, "that were the narrorest shave of doonright decappination ah've ever had. Oi wonder 'ow those other fellows a' git on?"

Big Budget 147; 7 April 1900 (H. O'Neill)

'Weary Willie and Tired Tim' took the air by balloon (p. 99) and the newfangled flying machine (p. 100). The invention of the cinematograph was immortalised by H. O'Neill's countryman-about-town, 'Uncle Greengage', who reacted as did Monsieur Lumière's first startled audience. The annual holidays were always celebrated in the comics, none more so than Christmas. Ally Sloper published his *Christmas Holidays* (p. 102) as a bumper special, extra to his weekly edition. Other comics doubled, even tripled, their standard eight-page issues.

Ally Sloper's Christmas Holidays

1887.] CONDUCTED BY GILBERT DALZIEL. [TWOPENCE.

BOXING-DAY AT ALLY'S.

"*At an early hour on Boxing-Day, Poor Papa, with his usual Yule-Tidish and Wassail-Bowlish magnanimity, distributed to the tradesmen of our neighbourhood what is known as 'The Sloper Bounty.' As you all probably know, this Bounty takes a different form each Christmas. Last year, for instance, the festive whelk was generously circulated; this year the succulent sausage was given away with reckless irresponsibility to all who liked to come to Mildew Court.*"—TOOTSIE.

Ally Sloper's Christmas Holidays; December 1887 (W. F. Thomas)

Comic Cuts 32; 20 December 1890

OUR·MERRY·XMAS·NUMBER·ONE·HALFPENNY·ONLY

The Halfpenny Comic ½

No. 151. Vol. VI.]   WEEK ENDING DECEMBER 8, 1900.   [ONE HALFPENNY.

BLINKER AND FUZZY-WUZZY DO THE GIDDY GHOST TRICK ON CHRISTMAS DAY.

1.—Hon the nite ov Xmas Eve Fuzzy-Wuzzy, mi slaive, and Hi (Blinker) determined 2 do grate deeds—a serting 'aunted 'ouse 'ad bin loadid wiv grub 4 sum darin' swells 2 'ave thare Xmas dinner thare.

2.—So we thort we wood like 2 inwestigate the sed grub. Lord! thare woz lots ov it—turkeys, puddin', shampain, hyesters, and setterer! "Fuzzy-Wuzzy!" Hi gurgles, faintly, "this hiz parrerdice at larst!"

3.—Then Hi 'ad a hidea. "Wiv this yere boar's 'ead," Hi konfided 2 Fuzzy, "we will find the way 2 a slap-up, orlrite blow-out ter-morrer—bein' honly wunst a year!" Then we gouged 'out 'is heyes and put candles hinside. Nex day noboddy kood find ther boar's 'ead, but——

4.—When ther swells began 2 arrive, 4th kaim Blinker wiv the boar's yead on. *That korpsed the footman in livery, 'oo sker-eamed out, "The 'ouse is 'AUNTID!" and——*

5.—Nex' minit we woz chasin' them darin' swells all froo the grate park 2 the big gates—orl ov 'em screechin' and yellin' abart terruble ghostesses! Wot woz the sequel?

6.—Bliss and 'armony, o' course! Likewize prime wittles, wich woz heagerly partook ov by ther noble harmy ov tramps and hunwashed, wot the generus Blinker invited 2 partake ov 'is Xmas cheer. O, it woz a tuchin' site 2 see ther gratitood ov them winnin' tramps and 2 'ear them sorftly smile at thare good fortin'—so it woz! Tork abart a Merry Christmas——!

SPECIAL XMAS NUMBER
FUNNY CUTS
1D

No. 445. Vol. XXI.] Registered.   ONE PENNY.   [December 15, 1900.

BUTTERCUP AND DAISY LOSE THEIR CHRISTMAS PUDDING.

2.—Then our pals took the puddin' from the boy. Butter held it while Daisy biffed the kid over the nut with the basket. "Take that! you greedy boy," said Daisy. "Wot yer makin' a row erbout, a bit o' Christmas puddin' wot we want, eh?"

1.—'Twas Christmas Eve. The pals were sad, 'cos they didn't see how they were going to get any of the nice things people eat on Christmas Day. When suddenly they saw a boy coming towards 'em with a big basket on his arm, an' in that basket were a big plum-pudding. "We must 'ave that," hissed Buttercup. So they stopped the boy, an' Daisy—with a knife in his hand—said, "Hand over yer walliables." But the boy said he "Weren't a-goin' to give the puddin' to no one."

3.—The two chums then took the puddin' round the corner to examine it. When they uncovered it, it fairly made their mouths water; it looked grand. But hark! what are those voices round the corner? Daisy looked, what did he see? He saw the boy telling a bobby about the pals collerin' his puddin'. Quick as lightening Daisy picked up the stolen puddin' an' put it on the side of the gateway wall, where once there'd been a stone ball. The puddin' stuck there looked just like the missing ornament.

6.—What did their feelin's feel like? Instead of their puddin', they beheld two faces larfin' at 'em. "Want yer puddin'?" said one. "Well, we're a-goin' to sneak it this time," said the other. "Oh! crummie," yelled Daisy. "It's the COLOURED COMIC bounders, an' they've got our puddin'."

4.—The boy and the copper came up. "There's the fellers, Mr. Policeman," said the boy. "Now, wot 'ave you to say to this charge?" said the bobby to our friends. "Oh! Mr. Orsifer," exclaimed Daisy, "the wickedness of that 'ere boy to say we stoled 'is Christmas puddin'; we ain't seen him before in all our lifetime. "Well," answered the cop, "I'll 'ave to search yer pockets." So the pals had their pockets turned inside out, and, of course, nothing were found. "I told yer we 'adn't got it," smiled Daisy. An' the copper got so wild with the kid—

7.—Then, before Butter. and Daisy could recover theirselves, the COLOURED Comic coons bunked off with the puddin', leaving our poor pals done. "Oh, why aren't people honest?" wailed Butter. An' we ask, Oh, why!

5.—He started to kick him. "Take that, you young willian, a-tellin' lies about respectable gents a-pinching of your puddin'." An' that bobby did give the kid beans. An' all this while the whole plot had been seen by two fellers behind the wall. Reader! don't you know 'em? Of course you do, they are the COLOURED Comic fellers Dick and Dan. An' while the copper was amusing hisself, an' Buttercup and Daisy enjoying theirselves, Dan took the puddin' off the wall. When the policeman an' the boy went away, the pals turned round—

The Comic World

The Victorian world was an ever-expanding empire with the Queen a motherly hub. Beyond her bounds, foreigners were even funnier, and Ally Sloper loved to abandon his battered topper and drainpipes to dress up in some hilarious national costume or other. His broken German precedes 'Katzenjammer Kids' conversation by a decade. The international gathering around jolly John Bull for the first issue of *The World's Comic* (p. 107) is a splendid assembly of stereotypes. The funny Frenchman was also a popular butt, thanks to the Paris Exhibition (pp. 108–9), while the Russians provided Anarchists (p. 110) and the Czar himself (p. 111). Yankees were generally sharp con-men (p. 40).

AN EXCHANGE OF COURTESIES—AND DRINKS.

"It is not generally known, but for some considerable time past, Prince Bismarck and Poor Papa have been in daily communication with one another, when we read of the Prince's resignation in the Papers, none of us were at all surprised that Papa should run over to Berlin. Alexandry was appointed Pri *Secretary to the Conference which took place, and from him we hear that the crisis in Germany was never once alluded to, the one and only topic being Br* *Gin versus German Beer. Alexandry says that Poor Papa got the best of it, both in the quality of discourse and the quantity of refreshment."—Too*

Ally Sloper's Half-Holiday 311; 12 April 1890 (W. F. Thomas)

THE WORLD'S COMIC

EDITED BY ½D GRANDAD TWIGGLE

No. 1. Vol. I.] Registered. ONE HALFPENNY WEEKLY. [July 6, 1892.

JOHN BULL : "Laugh, I thought I should have died."
CANADIAN INDIAN : "Makes poor Indian laugh like rum and molasses."
FRANCE : "Eh, Alphonse, le journal pour rire n'est ce pas ?"
ITALY : "Saffron-hillo muchee grinna."
SCOTLAND : "Ey, mon ; but it's a reight gude ha'p'orth, ye ken."
NEGRO : "Golly ! dis am a gum-tickler."
AMERICA : "Say, old hoss, this is a screamer, you bet."
WALES : "Hur cannot help laughing at it, look you."
GERMANY : "Ze World's Gomeek. Yah, yah ! Better as goot."
IRELAND : "Hurroo ! This beats Bannagher, begorra."
CHINA : "Makee hi-tiddlee-hi-ti laughee tillee crackee sidee."

The World's Comic 1 ; 6 July 1892

THREE PAPERS FOR A PENNY!

The Big Budget. 1ᵈ

Are you trying for our
ONE WORD COMPETITION?

VOL. I. No. 6.　　　WEEK ENDING SATURDAY, JULY 24, 1897.　　　PRICE 1ᵈ

AIRY ALF AND BOUNCING BILLY GO TOURING IN FRANCE.

1. Airy Alf and Bouncing Billy embarked on the Marguerite bound for Boulogne. They were beastly ill all the way. "I wish I were 'ome," moaned Billy. "Get out ; yer sea-sick, not 'ome sick," spluttered Alf.

2. After landing at Boulogne they picked up a bit. "Naa we shan't Bou-long," says Airy Alf. "Here comes some of them ere fascinatin' fisher gals we've heard abart."

3. Airy Alf took a snap-shot at the group. "This is jest 'ow we likes it," gurgled Bouncing Bill.

4. But they didn't think much of it when two great burly fishermen came and smote them on the collar and cummerband, and finished up by—

5. Dropping them into the harbour. "This ain't no treat at all," moaned Billy, as he drank in a dozen 'arfs of sea water.

6. And as soon as they crawled out they were arrested by the gendarmes for bathing in prohibited waters.

Big Budget 6; 24 July 1897 (Tom Browne)

, SCENE THE ONTH.—The Paris Exhibition.—Enter two noble British figures. "Ah! there are. girls," tootled Duke Bertie Bounder, "I see yer. Meet yer later, duckies." "Pay 'eer," ked the gendarme at the gate. "Orl right, cocky," yapped Lord Algy, "I'll pay yer. There e. Come on, Bertie. Lead me to a refreshment bar. Rool Britannier, and down with nch beer."

2. Shortly after the two aristocrats were seated at a table surrounded by waiters. "Wilt quaff the flowing bowl with me, Dook?" quoth Lord Algy. "Odds bodikins," replied the Duke, "I will e'en take a mouthful at thy expense, fair lord." "No, yer don't," growled Lord Algy, "I'll stand a bottle and no more. Waitah! champagne, slave, an' don't blow the 'ead off it." "Oh, zese rich Eenglish," murmured the little French girls, "zey are so charming."

But, meanwhile, the two French Johnnies were getting a bit wild at the way the noblemen were hing their girls, and when they caught Bertie winking at them they got fairly mad. "Sacred !" they yelled, "zis ees an insult to France." "Oh, go and wash yerselves," piped the pals. -r-r-h! zey 'ave insult us once again. Zey say ve 'ave vash ourselves," shrieked Alphonse. evare!" screamed Henri, and they grabbed the two noblemen by the noses with a big grab.

4. Now, of course, no Briton, let alone a B.B.'ite, would let a Froggie pull his nose, and so in about half a minute there was one of the daisiest scraps going on you'd see in a lifetime. "Let 'im 'ave it, Bertie; goffer 'im! Smash 'im in the duff-box! Bang! Whoosh! Crack!" came from the centre of the crowd, mixed with bottles, bad language, and bits of Frenchmen.

And when the fight was over and it was quite safe to come near, two gendarmes came up and ched the Froggies off for assaulting two rich English lords. And, as the two wrecks were ied off to the prison hospital, a small, sad voice moaned "Mon Dieu, Alphonse, vot fools ve to touch ze Eenglishmen. Zey fight like devils." "Oh, give me back me right ear," ned Alphonse.

6. And then the lordlings mounted their trusty motor car and made off (with the girls, of course). "Fair damsel," simpered Lord Algy, "I love yer. Wilt marry me, and share me 'appy 'ome, and me hancestral 'alls?" "Vere are your—vot you say—hancestral 'alls?" asked the simple maid. "Oh—ah—down the Mile End Road, fust turning to the right, past the pub and there you are," guffed the haughty noble. And just then they passed the Froggies. "Solong, cockies," they laughed, "try tatcho for that bald patch on yer heads."

Big Budget 163; 28 July 1900 (Charles Genge)

GRAND VOTING COMPETITION. £25 AND 80 OTHER PRIZES.

The Big Budget 1d

YOU CAN WIN £25 BY A FEW SECONDS' WORK.

VOL. III. No. 55.   WEEK ENDING SATURDAY, JULY 2, 1898.   PRICE 1D.

ALF'S ANNARKIST CLUB.

1. They were broke and homeless. "Oh, for the ghost of a kipper's backbone," sighed the cat. Then Alf's mighty brain hit an idea. "Billy," he hollered. "I've got fourpence. Let's disguise ourselves and become anarchists."

2. It was done with a tanner subscription, and the shekels rolled in—so did the anarchists. Most of 'em had forgotten to wash their necks, but that didn't matter. "This is orfrite," laffed Billy.

3. Then Billy made a great speech. "Feller citizens," he hollered, "we are trod on like worrums by the orty rich. We will smack 'em back, and give 'em wot for with the secret bomb and the gory knife!" "'Ear, 'ear!" said the crowd.

4. Alf blotted the book and rose. "Tike the oath, comrades. Swear that you'll avenge yer wrongs; swear ter upset the happlecart of the bloated haristocrat." They swore.

5. But before this was half finished, the cops were on the job. That club was bust in about a second. Most of the anarchists hopped it, but Alf and Billy found their luck was out. They were nabbed.

6. "Come along, my little men," sniggered the orficer. "It's a nice 'ealthy ride, and we don't charge yer no fare. Jump in!" The bounders had got to. We expect they'll be out next week.

Big Budget 55; 2 July 1898 (Tom Browne)

THE ADVENTURES OF JIMMY JINGLE AND PETER PENLY.

THEY INTERVIEW THE CZAR OF RUSSIA.

"Here's a pretty jaunt for us," said Jingle; "a telegram from the Editor of *Comic Life*: 'Start at once and interview the Czar on the Peace Question.'" So they decided to disguise themselves as Russian noblemen and proceed at once.

The departure of Count Jimmyniski and Prince Peterova created quite a commotion in the street. Being in a violent hurry to catch the boat train, the driver of the motor-cab started before the Count could get inside.

Arrived at the Czar's palace, they lost no time in seeking an interview with his Majesty. "Bai Jove," muttered Prince P., "these uniforms *do* fetch 'em." "It's our commanding presence," answered the Count, as they passed the bowing flunkeys.

They very smilingly bowed to the Czar when he arrived, but when they introduced themselves and their mission they made rather a mess of it. "P-p-peace, your Majesty," stuttered Jimmyniski, "w-w-we've come to see you about the pleace proposals."

"Police proposals?" said the Czar. "Here, what's the meaning of this imposture? I believe you're Nihilists. Eject these ruffians at once, and cause their immediate arrest." And poor Jimmy and Peter were ignominiously ejected—

And marched off to the police cells. "This here's a pretty way to treat emissaries of peace!" said Peter. "When I get back to England I'll enter Parliament, and propose war with Russia at once." "Wait till you *get* back," moaned Jimmy. (*See how they escaped, in the next instalment.*)

THE SEASIDE SEASON IN COMIC CUTS COLONY

1. The seaside season is on in Comic Cuts Colony. The trains arrive every five minutes, and shoot the people out on to the beach.

2. The hotels are all full.

3. The elephant roundabout is well patronised.

4. Also the band—"The Musical Animals," conducted by Mr. Monkey.

5. The trained whale is doing a roaring business as a pleasure-boat.

6. One has a nasty trick of suddenly diving to the bottom, and upsetting the show. But the passengers are used to his little ways, and being good swimmers, generally manage to get back in time for tea.

The Funny Wonder 237; 14 August 1897

ve (catching sight of Churchwarden Choker, who
as a missionary): "A stranger? Good! De Spanish
ot away before I could steal his trowsers, but I
up for lost time." (Aloud.) "Delighted to meet
sah. Permit me to escort yo' to de hotel. Yes,
Ladrones. Spanish word, yo' know—means thief.
rds said we wuz all thieves, so we stole de name.

2. "Allow me to carry your bag, capting. And if yo' will
remove your coat and heavy shoes yo' will be much more
comfortable. It is so hot. Oh, no—no troubles at all to
carry zem!" And Choker innocently handed them over.

3. "That headland, majah, is Procrastination Point,
so called because it is de thief ob time. De view is so
enchanting, dat when yo' visit it, yo' linger for hours."
(Steals his watch.) "Silver watch? Rats!

w, honourable sah, if yo' will make yourself comfort-
r dis here nice shade, I will carry yo' tings to de
send a carriage for yo'. It's a tiresome walk."
y," thought Choker, "the natives here are most

5. Shortly afterwards Choker was disturbed by a gent
with a formidable-looking walking-stick. "'Scuse me,
sah, but dey's a fellow up at de hotel sez yo' held him up,
an' robbed him ob his jewellery, clo'es an' money, an' dere's
a gang comin' down to finish yo' off. Gimme dem pants
yo's got on, an' skip while yo's got de time.

6. "Run, sah, run! Dere's a hundred years in gaol
for any stranger caught stealin' in dese islands. I'll
let yo' keep de umbrella—takin' an umbrella ain't
stealin' anyway, even in de bes' society." Then
Churchwarden Choker made a bolt for his boat.

Comic Cuts 444; 12 November 1898

'The Comic Cuts Colony' was first colonised by *Comic Cuts* on 10 November 1894: four pictures described the Great Mushroom Development. The Colony ran irregularly for years, introducing such occasional characters as 'Smirk the Elephant Detective', a parody of the paper's fictional feature, 'Dirk the Dog Detective'. The series grew so popular that on 4 May 1895, all the comic's strips and cartoons took place in the Colony! Later the C.C.C. overlapped into *Comic Cuts*' companion, *The Funny Wonder* (p. 112). Blackamoors were always good for a laugh, and were popular butts in other strips, such as 'Churchwarden Choker'.

The Big Budget 1d

LAST WEEK OF £25 COMPETITION.

VOL. II. No. 46.   WEEK ENDING SATURDAY, APRIL 30, 1898.   PRICE 1D.

BOUNCING BILLY AND AIRY ALF, THE EXPLORERS, HAVE A NARROW ESCAPE.

1. A. A. and B. B. accidentally struck a noted tribe of cannibals, the terrible Missionary-shifters. "Time to go," said AM. "So I grees," sighed Billy. They goed.

2. But those niggers could sprint a bit, so the unlucky pair shinned up a couple of palm trees. And d'n't those nigger boys laugh 'us! They got the axes to work, an'!——

3. Splosh! Somebody got rather wet, you bet on it. "Oh, oh," gurgled A f, "this is wot I calls rude." Billy thought of happy, happy Camberwell, and sighed a big sigh.

4. And then the cannibal boys hooked 'em out of the waves, and carted 'em off on the royal giraffe to the King's missionary grill at Rotlemaloo. "I've known funnier things than this," mused Billy. "Oh ———— a thing it is to weigh eighteen stun!"

5. It happened that the old King was a beggar for curries, and he always made a point of putting the spice in the pot him off. This took a bit of time, which was lucky for A. A. and B. B. For——

6. Just then an old-man rhinoceros happened to strol by, and thought he'd call in at the palace. He did. N.B.—The dinner was postponed.

Big Budget 46; 30 April 1898 (Tom Browne)

1. "Jee-crikey!" smiled Chowgli, "if dat ain't de biggest winkle I nebber seed!" "Him must hab 'scaped from Barnum's," added Stripes. "Let's take 'im 'ome."

2. So, with a few bits of twine, they harnessed that snail, and got on its back. "Golly!" said the kid, "dis ain't no 'spress train; but 'im goes up hill well."

3. When it took to going up the side of the cliff, though, the little pals were hardly so comfortable. "Somebody git me a bit ob resin, me hands so slipperly!" yelled Chowgli.

4. He didn't require it, though, for the kid managed to grasp that motor-car's rudder. "Dis am a little bit ob nice," said the tiger. "So-so!" answered the Kid. "Take you finger-nails out ob me weskit—dey tickle."

5. But soon afterwards the snail had that tired feeling, and drew in its head and tail to have a snooze. "Berry rude to go to sleep when you got company!" screamed the Kid, as he and Stripes left rather sudden for the earth. "Dis will hurt our feelings."

6. But it didn't, for their fall was broken by two of Mrs. Greaterouselbird's eggs. "Lawks!" it said, "me hab hatched some chicks in me time, but dese two tings take de onion. Me not going to lay no more eggs."

Illustrated Chips 467; 12 August 1899

The opening up of Africa provided plenty of fun and some serial-like adventure for Willie and Tim and Alf and Billy (p. 114). The *Big Budget* boys were usually found in that unlikely area of Africa, Beebeeland, clearly a near neighbour of the C.C.C., as Comic Cuts Colony was colloquially called. The first Negro hero was the well-drawn 'Chowgli', out of Mowgli by Little Black Sambo, who shared jungle fun with Stripes the tiger from 21 January 1899.

1. "DEAR MR. EDITOR,—I still find dis de most obligin' country in de world. De kindness ob yo Blitish people is simply hebbenly! Fo' instance, de way yo pervide nice cool drinks in de streets for de wayfarers and odder people who am dry is weally lubly. Wo! Me takee dis idea back to China certingly fo' suah! I muchee pleased at Blitish thoughtfulness. Again, Mister Editor——

2. "Oh, de lubly music in de streets! And de obligi[n] young ladies who askee me to dancee wid dem! I enjoy d[e] sort ob ting better dan a plate of boiled puppy wid sna[il] fritters around de edges. Wo! It am glorious! De youn[g] misses who dancee am so pleasant and kind.

3. "And also, Mister Editor, how kind is de people around Petticoat Lane, hey? I buy one nicee new top-hat fo' two-poun'-ten (dat was made for de Prince of Wales, only it didn't fit proper), and dey den makee me one big present ob a suit ob clothes! Wo! A present fo' nodding—just because I buy one ob de Prince's silk hats! How kind an' simple dese people are, hey? Wo!

4. "But de ting dat impress me most wuz de respect ob [de] people when dey see me wid my new Blitish clothes o[n]. Dey cheer, and smile loud, and clap me on de back, a[n] hooray! Sez I, dey take me for de Prince ob Wales, becau[se] ob dis hat ob his! I do not undeceive dem, but let dem che[er] me still muchee! It wuz grand, Mister Editor, and I rea[lly] proud ob de English people. I really am. Wo! I much[ee] flattered. — Your hebbenly chop-chop, MISTER GEOR[GE] WUN LI."

Big Budget 180; 24 November 1900 ('Jan')

The Victorian Oriental was not yet the Yellow Peril, and the Cheery Chink and the Jolly Jap were interchangeable objects of amusement. Naturally, the Heathen Chinee was the funniest, because he had a pigtail, although the Boxer Rebellion made him a little less laughable (p. 142). High caste Indians were funnier than low[er] (p. 117), and the Discovery of the Pole was pie to the likes of the rival tramps (pp. 118-19).

LOOK INSIDE FOR OUR GRAND NEW STORY, "THE KING OF KLONDIKE."

The Funny Wonder

EIGHT LARGE PAGES,

1d. 1/2

No. 263. Vol. XI.   ONE HALFPENNY. EVERY SATURDAY.   February 12, 1898.

HOW RAJAH JAHMRANJEE REGAINED HIS SON AND HEIR.

1. While Yummisweet, the nurse, was out with the Rajah's son and heir the other day she met a chap that she was sweet on. "Good-morrow, dear," remarked the chap; "the morn is almost as sweet and gracious as thyself. "Oh, go hon!" she smirked shyly. "You don't say so!" But in the meantime Jolop, the black boy, was busily engaged, as you will see.

2. When Yummisweet found she had lost the kid, she went to the Rajah, and tore her hair a bit. "Oh, my lord! my lord!" she said, "thy child hath been pinched!" "W-hat!" yelled the Rajah. "Base woman, thou shalt be slain if he is not found."

3. But before getting on with the slaying, the Rajah thought of the elephant. "Tuski," he said brokenly, "my child hath been nicked! Find him, and your grub allowance shall be doubled." "I will," sobbed Tuski.

4. For many hours the faithful animal mouched round, and at last he came across Jolop and his pal, who were treating the son and heir to a little gentle exercise. "What ho!" murmured Tuski; "I fancy I'm in this."

5. And the joy of the loving father, when his offspring was brought back by Tuski, was too deep for any words except Indian ones—which you wouldn't understand. Poor old Jolop wasn't quite so delighted, though; and neither was his pal.

6. "Ah!" murmured the Rajah a little later, "this is something like. How do you like it, boys? Mustard's a very fine thing, you know. Don't you think so?" The boys certainly differed from the Rajah, but they were too much occupied to say so. Tuski, however, felt pleased with himself, and Yummisweet was happy.

The Funny Wonder 263; 12 February 1898 (Tom Browne)

The Big Budget 1ᵈ

Over £30 Worth of Prizes.
LOOK INSIDE.

VOL. IV. No. 85.   WEEK ENDING SATURDAY, JAN. 28, 1899.   PRICE 1D.

AIRY ALF AND BOUNCING BILLY VERY MUCH UP THE POLE.

1. "ALF," simpered Billy, "balloons ain't no use ter find the Pole, and ships is right orf. This is the only way ter do it. Gee-hup! Give 'em sum gruel!"

2. But the gruel upset the team, and they biffed right up against the true pole, an' only jenniwin Norf Pole. Hooray! At last they had found it—but where was Alf?

3. Explorers are a trifle tough, and Billy soon got over the shock. "Look 'ere, Tom Pussy," he warbled, "I'm goin' ter show yer 'ow the oily Esquimaux cops the slimy little sealet, see?"

4. "Oh, Pip! Likewise Green Geraniums and Odiferous Eau-de-Cologne! My whiskers," murmured the tyke, "ain't this a funny country, catty?" It wasn't a seal—it was Alfie.

5. For a bit all was joy. But if you think Alf and Billy were going all the way to the Pole for nothing you're a bit orf it. "Whoosh!" panted Alf, "hit him again."

6. And Billy got his colossal muscle on the go, and kerash went the old North Pole. Then they started for Maiden Lane; and the cat said: "Just look at me."

Big Budget 85; 28 January 1899 (Ralph Hodgson)

HOW D'YE DO?

HAB A LOOK AT PAGE 4!

No. 528. VOL. XXI. (New Series.) [Entered at Stationers' Hall.] PRICE ONE HALFPENNY. [Transmission Abroad at Book Rates.] OCTOBER 13, 1900.

WEARY WILLY AND TIRED TIM AT THE NORTH POLE.

1. Sit tight and draw your breath hard! The things in the picture are not dangerous, if you don't annoy 'em. You see, Willy and Tim were panting with a very deep pant after something exciting; and, as they wanted to be as far away from a police-station as possible as well, they just rigged themselves up with a brand-new motor-car, fitted with a cow-and-dog-catcher, and started for the North Pole. "By-by! tooraloo!" sang Willy from behind. "See you when we come back!" "Don't be long!" wept the girls; "we shall be so lonely without you two nice men. Booh-ooh!"

2. Then away went the merry pair, and travelled and travelled till they got among the icebergs. "Pip-pip!" shouted Willy to the French explorers in the sledge. "We're Roberts and Kitchener on the biffbash for the Pole, to see if there are any Boers about; so please be respectful!" "That's it, Willy," chirped Tim; "dig it into 'em! I can see you getting a thump in the lug before you're much older!" Willy's reply melted a lot of the ice; but the motor went straight on, as if nothing had been said.

3. Pretty presently they got off to have a liker at what was which, and, if so, why. "Tim!" jerked out Willy, "there's some nasty, low-minded, jealous folkses been sneaky enough ter discover the Pole before us!" "It do seem so," agreed Tim. "The warmints! But wos Willy and Tim ever done by jest a handful of explorists? Nay; let us wipe them off the earth!"

4. Whizz! Whurróo! "Pip-pip! Hi-hi!" shouted Tim, as he ran the motor up against their tender parts. "Gerrout the way! D'yer wanter be run over—careless?" "See?" interrupted Willy; "that's wot you git fer bein' tricky!" And he gave a pathetic address to the people in the air, just like a real M.P. "This is where our patent cow-catching, pants-grabber attachment comes in handy!" smiled Tim. Then there were several dull, sickening thudlets, and all was quiet.

5. Of course those chaps were too biffed-up to carry on about it; so the pals gently but firmly collared the North Pole. "This don't seem a werry lovely thing ter come so far arter!" grumbled Willy. "And it are heavy, too!" "Comorfit!" chuckled Tim; "it's worth it. Hold yer end up, Willy boy, and don't let all the weight on yer pore pal's shoulders!" So they trotted along till they got to Klondike—the place where people find themselves there's gold—and—

6. Set up a barber's shop. "'Ere y'are, toffs and noblemen!" shouted Willy. "Come and be the only and fustest ter have a shave under the North Pole!" "Yus," put in Tim, "a clean shave fer five quid a time—and a toy to the best-behaved gents! Now, walk up—do, afore we git generous, and raises the price!" And those Klondikers just moseyed up and paid. Then the pals sold 'em the North Pole at a bargain, and came home rich.

Illustrated Chips 528; 13 October 1900

The Comic War

The comic war fought between Alfred Harmsworth's Pandora Publishing Company, James Henderson, George Newnes, C. Arthur Pearson, and Trapps, Holmes & Co, was serious business compared with the real thing—as fought on the funny pages. Ally Sloper had been Special War Correspondent for *Judy* in the Franco-Prussian War of 1870, and now that he had his own weekly *Half-Holiday*, naturally he was ready, aye, ready (p. 120). *Comic Cuts* was first to the front with a Grand Military Number (p. 121), and Tom Browne's Alf and Billy, being bicyclists, were quick to join the Volunteer Cycle Scouts (p. 122). They were the first of the few Britons to rush to Uncle Sam's aid in the Spanish–American War (pp. 123–6), and first to take Fashoda in Victoria's own Boer War (p. 127). Their many adventures with Oom Paul were capped only by their old rivals, Willie and Tim, who took Pretoria personally on 21 April 1900 (p. 140).

SLOPER AT THE MILITARY EXHIBITION.

"*At the special request of the Committee, Poor Papa honoured the Royal Military Show at Chelsea with his presence the other day. He was accompanied by Mamma, who was awfully sweet as a vivandiere, after the style of Mabel Love, in 'Faust Up to Date.' Papa was perhaps a little too military, but it's all a matter of taste. The Prince of Wales and the Duke of Cambridge received the visitors, and escorted them round the Exhibition. Ma says at times Cammy was quite skittish. Papa says Albert Edward was awfully tickled with a wheeze he told him about Henry of Battenberg. Papa has not told me.*"—TOOTSIE.

Ally Sloper's Half-Holiday 318; 31 May 1890 (W. F. Thomas)

OUR MILITARY NUMBER.

THE "MARVEL"
GRAND
DOUBLE XMAS
1d. NUMBER 1d.
Now on Sale.

Comic Cuts.

½d.

ONE HUNDRED LAUGHS FOR A HALFPENNY.

No. 346. Vol. XIV.] Registered.   ONE HALFPENNY WEEKLY.   [December 26, 1896.

WHO DID HE MEAN?

Officer : "Private Smith, the sergeant says you used insulting language towards him !" T. A. : "I did not, sir. I simply said some of us here ought to be in a menagerie !"

ON PARADE.

Officer : "What do you mean by coming on parade in that state, sir? Why, you haven't shaved, you dirty fellow !" Soldier : "If yer please, sir, I'm growing my whiskers." Officer : "Oh, you are, are you ? Well, you've plenty of time to do that off parade. I'd strongly advise you to shave 'em off before you come on. Two days' pack-drill !"

FROM THE RAW MATERIAL.

'Arriot : "Lor' ! Bill, I don't 'ardly 'no' yer—yer looks ser bloomin' smart !"

THE ASSASSIN BRAND

Warranted to kill at 1,000 yards !

TOMMY ATKINS AND JOHN BULL.

John Bull : "Tommy, old chap, I'm proud of you ! We joke at you sometimes, but we'd be a long way behind without you !"

TOMMY IN THE WARS AGAIN.

1. Maria says, "Go into the garden, Bill, till I've washed up, and I'll meet you there."

2. Sproggins (on the other side of the wall) : "What, that darned skunk of a cat out there again !

3. "I'll give her a skewallop this time, and no mistake !"

4. Tommy thought he was going through Tel-el-Kebir again !

Comic Cuts 346; 26 December 1896

SPECIAL BANK HOLIDAY NUMBER.

The Big Budget. 1d

Are you a Member of
the B.B.B.? *See page 2.*

VOL. I. No. 7.   WEEK ENDING SATURDAY, JULY 31, 1897.   PRICE 1D

AIRY ALF AND BOUNCING BILLY BANK HOLIDAY MAKING.

1. Airy Alf and Bouncing Billy, being both loyal volunteers, ride to review. "These togs fetch the girls," sings Alf, as they wink at the passers-by.

2. On arriving on the field of action, they are told off as scouts. "Wot's a scout?" asks B.B. "Don know," replies Airy Alf; "let's go off and find out."

3. A.A. and B.B. go off and hide behind a tree in a wood. "'Ere comes the henemy, Alf; let fly."

4. They both shoot; but the enemy turns out to be two gamekeepers, who, thinking they are dealing with poachers——

5. Go for Airy Alf and Bouncing Billy.

6. And this is the condition they were in when they reached camp.

Big Budget 7; 31 July 1897 (Tom Browne)

The Big Budget 1d

FANCY MEETING YOU!

VOL. II. No. 49.   WEEK ENDING SATURDAY, MAY 21, 1898.   PRICE 1D.

AIRY ALF AND BOUNCING BILLY WANT TO FIGHT THE SPANIARDS.

1. When Alf and Billy, on full war-paint, strolled into Washington, they fairly astonished the Yankees. "I'll bet Spain'll get the collywobbles now," said Alf. "You bet," snorted Billy.

2. Then they dropped in to see Mr. McKinley. "'Ow goes it, old hoss?" chort of Alf; "we've come ter volunteer ter bust the Spaniards." Billy was sampling the Scotch. "That's so," he gurgled.

3. But when they hinted to the President that they wanted to be made generals on the spot, there was a bit of a shindy. Those Yankee peelers are hot stuff. "This way out here," they said.

4. "Seems ter me," sighed Billy, "they've been very rude ter us. I reckon this flag'll make 'em wild, eh?" There can be no doubt about it—it did.

5. And in less than a millionth of a minute things began to get warm. "The vulgar wretches," panted Alf; "they ain't got no hideer of perliteness." Billy said nix. It took him all his time to run.

6. The chase grew hotter and hotter. "We're deaders for a quid," moaned A. A., when revolvers began to follow the bricks and cats. But Alf was mistook, for just then the British Consulate came in sight. It was a near thing, though, you bet.

Big Budget 49; 21 May 1898 (Tom Browne)

The Big Budget. 1d

ISN'T THIS A SPLENDID NUMBER?

VOL. II. No. 50.   WEEK ENDING SATURDAY, MAY 28, 1898.   PRICE 1D.

AIRY ALF AND BOUNCING BILLY RUN THE BLOCKADE.

1. To get even with Mr. McKinley, Alf and Billy decided to run the Cuban blockade. "Don't this jest remind yer of Margit?" chortled Alf, as he paced the deck of the *Saucy Shrimp*. Billy scanned the horizon. "By gum, there's a ironclad!" he yelled.

2. It wasn't, though. It was only a vessel with a cargo of Spanish nuts. But when night fell (it falls with a bump in them parts), an American cruiser turned on the limejooce. "See me biff her," laughed Alf. "We are discovered."

3. Boom! C-rash! That Yankee ship biffed first with a shell that startled the blockade runners a bit. "W-o-o-o-o!" shrieked Billy. "These things *can* bite!" "Never mind," roared Alf. "Just wait till I come down."

4. Both the *Saucy Shrimp* and the bold blockade-runners were looking a trifle the wuss for wear when Alf ran his eye along that gun. "I'll blow that ship ter Klondike," he lisped. "Don't tork," said Billy. "Fire!"

5. And Alf fired. "Seems ter me," remarked the shark to his pal, "there's something coming our way at last. Wunnerful inventions them torpeeders. I'm on that fat bloke wen 'e drops. What ho!"

6. But did those sharks dine off Alf and Billy? Oh no, not a bit! They'd only got to swim ashore, and, when they crawled out and told the Spaniards they'd run the blockade, there were high jinks, you bet. They're going to get a pension now. Hurroo!

Big Budget 50; 28 May 1898 (Tom Browne)

NEW HAIR RESTORER COMPETITION
The Big Budget. 1d

TWO BICYCLES FOR WEARY READERS.

Vol. II. No. 51.　　WEEK ENDING SATURDAY, JUNE 4, 1898.　　PRICE 1D.

AIRY ALF AND BOUNCING BILLY ARE SENTENCED TO DEATH.

1. " BLOOMIN' queer country this Cuba, ain't it ? " sighed Billy. " Blessed if I'd ever 'ave smoked a Havana cigar if I'd knowed where they came from." Alf wasn't in a very good temper. " Don't these cast-iron saddles cut some ? " he moaned.

2. And then they reached the bridge which you probably noticed in the first picture. That bridge struck at Willyam's weight, and there was a bust. " Tell muvver I died a 'ero's death," sobbed Alf, as they flew downwards. " Oh-o-ooh ! "

3. When the shadows were falling, two drenched and ragged wrecks limped into the Spanish camp. " Sapristi ! " bellowed Don Antonio Sopentripo, the Spanish general. " Yankee spies, by the joocy onions of Spain ! Seize 'em, camarados ! "

4. It was no use trying to b'uff old Sopentripo, for he was all there. Alf and Billy were roped up, an' the Don yelled : " Present ! " " Yer don't 'appen ter know wot won the Derby, old 'un ? " inquired Billy. " Don't tork," said Alf. " Die like a Briton."

5. But, luckily for Big Budgetites, Alf and his pal were as good as fifty dead men. Some of those Cuban insurgents were knocking about, looking for a place to get some mild and bitter. Bang ! Bang ! Cr-ack ! Those Spaniards got it hot.

6. " Our lodger's such a nice young man ! " chortled the brace of bounders, joyfully hugging those greasy insurgent chaps. " Oh, I say, this is all right ! If you'd come a bit later you would have been too late for tea." And all was peace.

Big Budget 51 ; 4 June 1898 (Tom Browne)

NEW HAIR RESTORER COMPETITION

The Big Budget. 1d

TWO BICYCLES FOR WEARY READERS.

VOL. II. No. 52.   WEEK ENDING SATURDAY, JUNE 11, 1898.   PRICE 1D.

AIRY ALF AND BOUNCING BILLY, THE SPIES, SCOOP THE BOODLE.

1. "PRISONAIRS," said the Spaniard, "you must work ze balloon or a–die! Here is–mooch gold, and here is lead. Vich vil you have?" Alf and Billy voted for the oof in a breath. "Potter out," they grinned.

2. And as the balloon drifted through the moonlight towards the American camp, a muffled voice inquired: "Say, Alfy, ain't these smokes all right?" "Prime!" said Alfy. "Good fun this spy bizness, eh?"

3. When the pale dawn broke, they found themselves spotted by the enemy. "Bet I knock a hole in that fat Johnny," said Alf. "Don't kill anybody yet. Give 'em time ter read the hand-bills," roared Willyum.

4. But the enemy chipped in with a shell which had a very spiteful way about it. "Oh, for the wings of a turtle-dove!" hollered Billy. Alf thought ditto, but said nix.

5. With their usual luck the bounders struck a tree and clung to it like limpets. "Them chaps'll get 'eartburn if they run like that," sniggered Billy. "Let's slither down and find some grub."

6. They slithered. And while the enemy was balloon-chasing they had a high old time in their camp. "Seems ter me," cooed Alf, as they toddled off with the swag, "those Yanks'll know we've been here." "I guess," lisped Willyum. "Wot luck!"

Big Budget 52; 11 June 1898 (Tom Browne)

The Big Budget. 1d

Vol. III. No. 70.   WEEK ENDING SATURDAY, OCT. 15, 1898.   PRICE 1D.

AIRY ALF AND BOUNCING BILLY TAKE FASHODA.

1. When the Sirdar sent back all the war correspondents, Alf and Billy objected. "Look here, Willyum," lisped Alf, "the Big Budget's goin' ter 'ave some news from the front." "Ree-ight-o!" said Billy. "I'm game. Gee hoop, me Arab steed."

2. But when those camels streaked straight for Fashoda with the patent sea-sick sixpence-a-sail trot, the bounders objected again "Drop it, yer double-'umped, frog-faced switchback," roared Alf And Billy gurgled piteously; "Oh, me pore bones."

3. Of course those "ships of the trackless desert" couldn't stand such language. They promptly wrecked themselves, and the crew got washed overboard. Bump! Billy struck the sand. Thump! Alf did likewise. "Enough ter give a billiard-table the hump, ain't it?" gurgled Billy.

4. The camels had strolled back to Khartoum for tea, so the dauntless ones had to foot it to Fashoda. They reached it and rang the bell. "Vat you vant?" hollered a voice. "We've come ter stay a week, old French polish," lisped Alf and Billy. "Open the door."

5. But those Fashoda gents weren't having any, and Alfie and Willyum got mad. Alf made a speech, while Billy, who's a champion at the game, picked the lock. Then they hopped in and made things hum. "Big 'un," shrieked Billy. "Kokernut or cigar, sir. Good shot!"

6. In about two ticks and an eighth Fashoda was taken. Next day the Sirdar turned up. "Wot cheer, 'Erbert," sniggered the town-takers, "we've got a little present fer yer—caught 'em orf ours 1vee. If yer don't make us dooks yer're no class." Strangely enough the Sirdar didn't seem to like it.

Big Budget 70; 15 October 1898 (Ralph Hodgson)

The Big Budget. 1d

Don't forget your "LENO"
on Tuesday.

VOL. IV. No. 90.　　　WEEK ENDING SATURDAY, MARCH 4, 1899.　　　PRICE 1D.

AIRY ALF AND BOUNCING BILLY PLAY THE DREYFUS GAME.

1. The French Johnnies saw last week's B.B., and decided to bribe Alf and Billy to sell them plans of the Camberwell fortifications. "Wotto, mongsoo," pipped Billy. "Make it another fifty and we'll chuck in a plan of Lord Wolsey's dorg-kennel!"

2. But, alas! while those Johnnies were chortling, and A.A. and B.B. were jingling those quidlets, a squad of the Camberwell Brigade bust in. "Wot's this?" they shrook. "Spies, eh? We harrest yer, thank yer, so come along."

3. They didn't want to go, but that squad had a nasty way about it, and was very rude. And Alf murmured: "Billy, me boy, this is again a promotion job, ain't it."

4. When they toddled into the barracks the secret information was fished out. Fished is the kerrect word, for it was kinder fishy and catty too. "Betr-r-rayed!" howled the Frenchies. "Givvus back our oof."

5. But when the Budget boys hook on to anything good, they don't part in a hurry. "Wotcher take us for?" they purred. "'Ere, take yer luggage, an' git." They got in a bit of a hurry.

6. And, later on, the Colonel said: "Me lads, you are a credit ter the Camberwell Brigade, and an honour ter the army. Thus do I pin these me'als on yer manly buzzums." "Thanks, old cook," sniggered the pair. "Steady 'ow yer does the pinnin'."

Big Budget 90; 4 March 1899 (Ralph Hodgson)

Crammed with funny pictures and grand stories.

The Big Budget. 1d

Vol. V. No. 124.   WEEK ENDING SATURDAY, OCTOBER 28, 1899.   Price 1d.

AIRY ALF AND BOUNCING BILLY CAPTURE KRUGER AND GENERAL JOUBERT.

1. "Morning Joe," said Billy. "How's the Missus? Me and my pal 'ere, Mister Airy Alf, late of the London Bridge Rifles, is jist off to capchur ole Kruger and General Joobert. We leeves the reward to you." And Chamberlain said: "Bring 'em back, and I'll give you a thousand quid each, and stand you an eel-pie supper."

2. 'Twas night, and Weary Tim and Tired Willy slept peacefully, after a hard ten minutes' work. "Don't they look bou-ti-ful?" murmured Alf. "Loverly," chirped Billy. "It's a pity we've got to disturb 'em, but it must be done. Git the ropes and the masks ready." Wot ho! the plot unfolds, dear reader.

3. Quickly the deed was done. "Hullo," pipped the crowl. "Wot 'ave yer got in that barrer?" And when the immortal pals told 'em it was Kruger and Joobert—well, we never did see such excite nent. "Billy," choked Alf, "it is the proudest moment of our lives." "Joe must git us a job in the Kabinit for this," answered Billy.

4. "Thank ye, Joe," chortled the pals. "We 'ad a fearful job to capcher 'em. We was fighting fer three hours and a quarter before we knocke l 'm out wiv a whack under the bodega. Keep 'em safe, specially old Kruger. He's very lot, he is. Sorry we can't stay to tea."

5. Then the Budget Boys vamoosed into the outer world, and Joe cut the cords that tied up Kruger and his pal, and—— "Great pip!" said the one and only Chamberlain, "I've been done." And Weary Tim and his pal broke into language that made the cat's hair curl.

6. "The next time," cooed the bobby, "that you come 'e e an' pass yerselves orf as Kruger and Joobar, you won't git treated so lightly." "Willy," moaned Tim, "it's those Budget fellers agin." But Willy only looked for a soft place to fall on, and found it not. And two voices over the fence murmured : "Say, cookies, do yer orlways come out like that?"

Big Budget 124; 28 October 1899 (Ralph Hodgson)

129

VOL. V. No. 125. WEEK ENDING SATURDAY, NOVEMBER 4, 1899. PRICE 1D.

AIRY ALF AND BOUNCING BILLY GIVE THE BOERS A GREAT FIREWORK DISPLAY.

1. It was the firework season, so the Budget boys thought they'd leave their rivals alone for a week and call on Kruger. "Wonder if the old cock will recernise us, Billy," chortled Alf. "Not 'im," purred Billy, who then addressed the crowd: "Now then, people, take yer seats, and don't forget to chuck yer money in the 'ats at the end of each display. English money only taken. None of yer own two pen'orth of silver to the arf-crown spondoolicks. Don't spit on the rockets, or you'll get chucked out."

2. Then the number one display was turned on, and Kruger and his pals were pleased muchly. "Goot—goot—darn goot!" they shouted. "Let us have twice some more." "Rightchar," cackled the pals. "The nex one is going to be a real good 'un—so don't fergit to get the cof re dy when we comes round wiv the colleckshun box."

3. "Alfred," spake Billy, "we are giving 'em a treat." "Don't they look pleased?" chirruped Alf. There was no doubt about it, too—they did enjoy it. Uncle Paul was so delighted tha' he borrowed a real English bob from General Joubert, and slung it into the hat. "And now me deer frends," chorussed the B.B. boys, "comes the great and final display which will conclude the evening's entertainment. Let 'er go."

4. And when Kruger and Company gazed upon this, the language almost put the fireworks out. "Vare is dose tam scoundrils!" yelled Paul. "Uncle," groaned the others, "dey haf bolted wiv der oof." "My bob's a goner," moaned Joubert. "I can never get it back from old Kruger." And later on the stars peeped down on a couple of flying forms. "We'll count up the chink at the next pub," wheezed Billy, "Wot a time we've had. It aint often you can do a Boer down for anything." "Not much," puffed out Alf. "If we don't get a medal each fer this, I'll never speak to Joe Chamberlin again."

Big Budget 125; 4 November 1899 (Ralph Hodgson)

A WONDERFUL LONG COMPLETE DETECTIVE STORY INSIDE.

The Big Budget. 1d

FULL OF COMIC PICTURES, STORIES & HELPFUL ARTICLES.

VOL. V. No. 127.   WEEK ENDING SATURDAY, NOVEMBER 18, 1899.   PRICE 1D.

AIRY ALF AND BOUNCING BILLY GIVE KRUGER AND JOUBERT ANOTHER SURPRISE.

1. THE pals are fairly on the war path now, and the British soldier boys (three cheers for 'em) won't think of parting with the B.B. boys. Last night the two unapproachables crept towards Kruger's camp, to see what they could do in the way of making things nasty for the Boers.

2. Uncle Kruger and nephew Joubert were fast asleep and dreaming about all the Britishers they were going to shoot down from behind nice big fat rocks to-morrow. "Bill," whispered Alf, "I've got an idea." "Ush," muttered Billy, "don't let old Kruger 'ear you, or he'll make you pay taxes on it."

3. "Now just fancy this dynermite and these 'ere pipes being left outside so careless like," chortled Alf, as he rammed another big dose home. "Yes, yes," purred Billy, "we shall have to teach 'm not to leave things about. Wot a nice comfy smoke the dear boys'll have when they wake up."

4. And while the pals hid behind the tent, Kruger and Joubert woke up and went to light up. "Ach," croaked Kruger, "next best to shooting a red-neck I do like a pipe of goot tobacco." And Joubert murmured, "I should say so, too. You are always porrowing one from me."

5. "Great Baden-Powell," yell'e Kruger, "vot is der matter vif der tam stuff?" And Joubert roared "dose kussed British they get everywhere. Dere is a kuppel of dem in mine pipe. Get out wif you——" But that dynamite was on business only, and before the Dutchmen could say "Oom Paul" there was a big—

6. BANG!—and two figures went up like the price of coals in winter. "It is dem Alf unt Beely vunts more," howled Kruger. But when the pals who were bolting with all the Boer war plans heard the language used by Joubert, they sadly sighed, "Oh, wot a norfully wicked man!"

Big Budget 127; 18 November 1899 (Ralph Hodgson)

THRILLING ADVENTURES OF BOUNDERBY BOUNCE, THE WAR CORRESPONDENT.
The Important Dispatch.

1. SINCE sending you my last graphic description of the magnificent victory which I achieved over a powerful Boer force last week, I have been specially selected, on account of the courage which I then displayed, to be the bearer of a most important dispatch. While the troops were eating a splendid Christmas dinner, I was sitting alone at a frugal repast. I scorn to eat while duty calls me. Suddenly, General Buller came into my tent. "Excuse me," he said, "I have here a very important communication to send to General White. I have chosen you, as the bravest man in the camp, to carry it. You may run terrible risks on the journey, but I know you laugh at peril. I can hardly bear to part from you, but duty is duty."

2. After a touching farewell, I left the General and commenced my preparations for the perilous journey. A magnificent steed had been selected for me. Some of the officers tried to persuade me to wear a suit of armour under my clothes. Of course, I scorned to take such care of my life. As I looked at the valuable dispatch I was to defend with my life, I lifted my head proudly, and glanced around with that eagle eye which has struck fear into so many Boers. The soldiers were dumb with admiration at my undaunted bearing. The whole camp turned out to see me off. With a large train of servants I started, amidst rousing cheers from the troops.

3. After many days travelling, I came within a short distance of my destination. The General had presented me with a very powerful telescope before I left, and, looking through this, I saw in the distance a large body of the enemy. Most men in my position would have fled, but not I. "Ha!" I muttered, "here is another chance to show my intrepid bravery. I will secrete myself, and endeavour to overhear the enemy's plans. Where danger lies, there is the heroic correspondent of the *Daily Shrieker*." My servants were trembling with terror——

4. And the whole body fled, leaving me and my faithful steed alone. With the dignity which always distinguishes me, I coolly dismounted, and, first seeing that my horse was safely hidden, I proceeded to take up a most dangerous position, right in the track of the advancing force. My first thought, of course, was for the valuable document on which so much depended. I could hear the enemy advancing close to me; the rattle of their arms and gnashing of their teeth were enough to have frightened many a brave man. But, as I have said, fear is unknown to me.

5. For a long time I heard them moving about in search of me, and I thought of the thrill of admiration which would run through the breasts of your readers as they hear of my daring exploit. Every moment I expected to be discovered, and knew that a terrible death awaited me if they detected my place of hiding. Please bear in mind that nothing but a sense of duty prevented me from springing out and slaying them. After a while, my horse sneezed and—we were discovered. Imagine my astonishment, as, with many bows and apologies, I was requested to come out by—the Boers?—no, by a party of British soldier boys. In my hurry, I had made a slight mistake. It wasn't the enemy after all.

6. Upon explaining that I was the bearer of an urgent dispatch, I was taken before the General. "This is a great honour, my boy," he said; "I have often heard of you, and longed to meet you. Come inside and have a drop of something warm." He then proceeded to open the letter. I cannot, of course, disclose the contents, which were of a very important nature, and referred chiefly to me, requesting that I should be handsomely rewarded. "I should like to give it to you myself, me boy," cooed General White. I am unable, at present, to mention the nature of the reward which I immediately received.

Big Budget 132; 23 December 1899 (Charles Genge)

THRILLING ADVENTURES OF BOUNDERBY BOUNCE, THE WAR CORRESPONDENT.

(Told by Himself and Illustrated by our own Truthful Artist.)

How he was Rewarded by Kitchener and Roberts.

1. Of course, by the time you receive this all England will be ringing with the news that there are now two other great men here besides me. Lord Roberts and Lord Kitchener have joined me. Special instructions were issued to the police not to allow any correspondents to be present at their arrival. Nevertheless, that low truth perverter, Yarnslinger, the war correspondent (ha, ha!) of the *Daily Shrieker*, determined to be there, and hid in a potato sack which was lying on the wharf. But I was there also. Yer faithful Bounderby had his eagle optic on the skunk. Yarnslinger snapped Lord Roberts just as he grasped Lord Kitchener's hand and cooed "Herbert, me boy, Bounderby, you and me'll just give those Boers socks, eh?"

2. At that moment I stepped forth. I could bear it no longer. I felt it was my duty to hand the mangy ink-slinger over to justice. Do not fancy that the fact that the ugly tramp has repeatedly insulted me had anything to do with my decision. The good of the country demands that the tyke shall be put out of the way. "Gentlemen," I crooned, "it is my painful duty to have to inform you that a spy is present. A French correspondent is concealed ——" "Where? Where?" shouted Kitchener, "let's have him shot at once." "Search that sack," I said sorrowfully, for my kind heart ached for the wretched Yarnslinger, scoundrel as he is.

3. In about two twos the soldier boys had the howling Yarnslinger out of his sack by the ear, and one of them proceeded to give him a coat of tar, to keep the damp out, as the two generals had decided to pitch him into the river. I stood and looked sorrowfully on, while Yarnslinger shrieked and raved. The villain dropped note books and cameras all over the place. The commanders were so enraged that they would have shot him at once, had I not brought my influence to bear upon them. I could not endure to see the wretched creature suffer the fate he so richly deserved.

4. "Now, boys" shouted Lord Roberts, "one, two, three, and away." And two Tommys heaved Yarnslinger into the water. "Oh, let me orf," he screamed, "I won't do it again. I will be good. The doctor said a bath would kill me." But in he went. What a contrast between this poltroon and your heroic correspondent. Had I been in his place I should have met my fate boldly and fearlessly, without a word. I have never known fear. But, there! we cannot all be brave. As I watched him I thought of the insults he had heaped upon me, and ——

5. Suddenly Lord Kitchener turned to me and said, "And who are you, sir, to whom we owe our lives? That noble face! I seem to have seen it somewhere. I cannot be deceived. Are you a prince in disguise, or only an earl?" "My lord," I answered, "you may have heard of me. I am the bravest, fiercest fighter in the British army. You have heard of the battles I have won, of the prisoners I have taken. My name is"—(and here I forgot Lord Kitchener's aversion to correspondents and gave myself away)—"my name is Bounderby Bounce. I——" "Wha-at!" shouted Kitchener, "Bounce, the distinguished war correspondent!!"

6. "You go after your pal." He was right. Just at that moment a last despairing wail came from the wretched Yarnslinger. Could I leave him to drown? No! Where danger is there am I. Kitchener was right. I would go after my pal! With one bold plunge I struck the water amid murmurs of admiration and rousing cheers. With tears in their eyes, both commanders themselves assisted me. After a fearful struggle with the rapid river (I was under water 37 minutes 26½ seconds at one time), I at last succeeded in rescuing the wretched Yarnslinger, amid the cheers of the soldiers on the wharf.

Big Budget 136; 20 January 1900 (Charles Genge)

£250 It's yours if you want it. See Inside. £250

The Big Budget. 1d

Get a copy of the "ILLUSTRATED WAR NEWS." Out to-day, price 1d.

Vol. VI. No. 137.   WEEK ENDING SATURDAY, JANUARY 27, 1900.   Price 1d.

AIRY ALF AND BOUNCING BILLY SELL KRUGER A NEW QUICK-FIRING GUN.

1. Oom Paul Kruger was in a bit of a fix. He wanted some more guns to whip the British (yes—he'll want a lot more for that), and there didn't seem much chance of getting any. "Donnerblitzen!" the old reprobate muttered, "ven dese confounded Britishers come to Pretoria, vot vil become of me?" And the nigger murmured under his breath: "Ole Buller him make it belly hot for you, me tink."

2. "Vot you say, my poys?" shouted Kruger. "Dis new gun vill fire ten tousand shots efery minnit. Mein Gott! it is sheap at der price." And Billy (er—we mean Colonel Von Sossiger) cackled: "Kruger, mein cocky, it's a bit of all right—made in Germany, and warranted not to bust if you treat it gently, and don't lean against it."

3. So Kruger handed over the thousand quidlets, and a Boer gent put a match to the gun just to see how she'd go. "Now then, gents," yell'ed Count Airy de Alfo, "keep your eyes on ze gun and watch him knock a chunk orf Ladysmith. Vaterloo avenged!" Then the two pals crept round to the rear so as the Boers could get a good look for their money.

4. Splutter—BANG!—fizz—BANG! BANG!—fizz—BANG! BANG!! BANG!!! Then the quickfirer started. And the Boers howled, "Oh, dake it away somevun. Ve're being killed all over!" And the voice of Alf from the back chuckled, "It's a good fing for us that we saved that cracker last firework day, ain't it Billy?"

5. BANG! WHOOSTER! FIZZ! CRACK! BANG-BANG-BANG-BANG! Still that quick-firing cracker cracked on. Oh, those Boers did have a time of it. "Der defil," yelled Kruger, "put up ze white flag." But the others moaned, "Ve can't uncle. Ve've run out of dem."

6. "Alfie," purred Billy, "fancy old Kruger giving a thousand quidlets for a common or garden cracker. Ain't it funny?" And Oom Paul used language that we can't print, really. "Dose Pig Pudget defils vunce more," he groaned, "1000 quids gone for ever, und now I shall have to vash meinself clean, und cover meinself vith sticking plaster. Vot a life, ain't it?"

Big Budget 137; 27 January 1900 (Ralph Hodgson)

OUR GRAND WAR NUMBER!   OUT ON THURSDAY, 28TH DECEMBER!   PRICE ONE PENNY.

ILLUSTRATED CHIPS 1D ½

SEE "OUR WAR STORY" or page 2

No. 486.   VOL. XVIII. (NEW SERIES.)   [ENTERED AT STATIONERS' HALL.]   PRICE ONE HALFPENNY.   [TRANSMISSION ABROAD AT BOOK RATES.]   DECEMBER 23, 1899.

THE NOBLE ARMY OF WEARY UNWASHED WANDERERS SPIFFLICATE THE BOER ARMY.

1. After their gallant exploits last week Willy and Tim hurried back to form a "Tramp Army" to take out to the Transvaal. And here they are enlisting the merry Out-of-work Brigade. "Now then, me 'andsome pal!" chirped Tim, "wot d'yer say to that? Free drinks, mind you!" "Free gargles!" whistled the Wanderer; "why I'd die twice a week for that!"

2. Such a tempting offer could not be resisted, and straight away the great Army of Weary Unwashed Wanderers was formed. "Now then, skinny Willy," quoth Tim, as he inspected the corps, "why can't you chuck a chest, and look proud?" "Carn't, old pal!" giggled Willy; "me muvver's sent it to the wash, and it ain't come back!"

3. So off they went on board their penny patent packet, and set sail for South Africa. "Great sea-serpents!" howled the fish; "wot a mob to worry me pore ole pal Kruger! This beats all the Dutch cheese I've ever smelled! Phew! Where's me scent-bottle?"

4. "At 'em, me brave army!" howled General Tim, "and don't forget to goffer 'em! Whir-oo!" "Woo-ough!" screamed the Dutchmen, "we can't fight these dirty coves! Hoist the flag of truce before we get a dig in the Orange Free State! Help! Murder! Tramps! Yow-ooh!"

5. But it was no go! The dusty Wanderers were on 'em before you could say "Glencoe," and jabbed the Boers all over the shop. "Wot the Bloemfontein are you up to?" howled the Dutch cornet, when Tim copped him one with his rusty blade. "That belongs to me, so stop hurting it when I tell you! Wow!"

6. That settled it. The Boers weren't game to tackle 'em again, so the Noble Army of Tramps marched into Pretoria. "Ah, Sir Reddy!" smiled Tim, "I think we've settled Mr. Kruger's hash this time! S'posing you 'ave a little sumfing with the toffs, and drink the health of the good ole British flag with cheers?"

(And they did, too; and if you take a peep at next Thursday's CHIPS' Special War Number, 1d., you'll see something worth seeing.)

Illustrated Chips 486; 23 December 1899 (Tom Browne)

The Big Budget. 1ᵈ

Our VALENTINE NUMBER.

VOL. VI. No. 140.   WEEK ENDING SATURDAY, FEBRUARY 17, 1900.   PRICE ONE PENNY.

AIRY ALF PLAYS A VALENTINE TRICK ON BOUNCING BILLY.

1. IN conserkwence of the wonderful way Billy managed to escape from Kruger last week, Buller has promoted him to be General Pawnbroker to the troops. He's been spending his time bossing Airy Alf (who is only a private), and cuddling a lovely little real jam puff in the town. "Popsy," Billy is saying, "look out for a ripping Valentine ter-morrer." And Airy Alf, who was listening, hissed: "I'll look cut fer it too!"

2. "Look here, young inkpot," whispered Alf, "'ere's four arf-do lars ter swop Valentines! Are yer on?" And the nig crooned: "Am I? Jest 'and over dem dollars, boss." And the deed was done, and the ooftish and the valentines changed hands. Ha! ha! Another deep plot. Pass on, please.

3. "Valentine from um General Billy de Bouncing One, Missy," smiled the nig. And the sweet girlet murmured: "What a dear boy to send me a Valentine. What is it, I wonder? Something awfully-awfully nice, of course." Now for a lovely——

4. *Surprise!!* Oh, dear! Oh, dear! You really wouldn't have thought that sweet girlet had such a temper. "You grinning little brute!" she shrieked, as she gave the nigger socks. "I'll teach your ugly master to send me a thing like this. The wretch! The horrid brute!! I'll Valentine him!!!!"

5. "Ow—yaw—wow!" yelled Billy. "Don't pull me lovely golding locks orl orf. Wot 'ave I bin and done? Ow—murder!" And the gentle girl hissed: "You'll send me another funny Valentine, will you? Whack! Bang!! Biff!!!" And Alfred the Airy tootled: "Her Pa must 'ave bin a chucker-out or a prize-fighter. Ain't the plot developing oririte?"

6. "Hand *that*," moaned Billy, "is the gal I spent me last two quid hon—the gal who to'd me she loved me 'cos of me wonderful likeness to Lord Kitchener? And nar she arf ke's me, an' goes orf with a feller who calls hisself a pal. Blowed if I ain't arf a mind to go 'ome and leave Lord Roberts to do the 'ole job wivvout me."—[Perhaps Billy will get over it by next week.—ED.].

Big Budget 140; 17 February 1900 (Ralph Hodgson)

1. ONCE again has your noble correspondent distinguished himself on the field of battle. One more glorious victory is added to the list of his brilliant successes. In an important engagement fought near here, I have again defeated the enemy, and taken a huge number of prisoners. General White found it necessary to send an important communication to Joubert, and requiring a person of unusual intelligence to be the bearer, he, of course, immediately decided to send me. But then, supposing I were sent, what would the garrison do without me, in the event of the enemy attacking Ladysmith in my absence? This consideration alone made me unwilling to set out, but I was at last *persuaded* to go, and the boys gave us a splendid send off.

2. The heat was terrific. The ground was so hot, that every time my foot touched it the boot-leather began to burn. In consequence of the awful heat, my head was fearfully swelled. [It's been like that a long time.—ED.] And my feet were so blistered that I was scarcely able to walk (the magnificent charger which the General had presented to me for the journey had been *burnt up* by the sun). At last we stopped to rest. I had some cold tea with me, but as there was only enough for one, I, with my usual generosity, gave it all to Inki. It was at this time that the scoundrel Yarnslinger, who had been following us, crept, unobserved, through the reeds behind me (as I was told afterwards), and stole the important letter, substituting for it one of his own.

3. Shortly after I arrived at the Boer camp, where I was received with great respect by General Joubert. It was curious to see the fear which my presence caused among the rascals. Drawing myself up to my full height, and casting around me a haughty glance from my eagle eye, I handed the letter to Joubert, I being ignorant, of course, of the dastardly treachery of the cowardly skunk who calls himself Yarnslinger. Joubert was in an extremely bad temper, having received a nasty message from Kruger, to the effect that unless he could do something better than hang about *outside* Ladysmith, he'd better chuck up his job. He held out a very dirty paw, and I passed over the letter to him.

4. He opened it and gave a frightful howl of rage. Yarnslinger had substituted for General White's letter one containing a valentine—a fairly truthful portrait of Joubert himself. "Donnerblitzen! Thunderweather!! Beeanskittles!!!" he roared. "This was meant to insult me, so it was. I let you know I'm Joubert, the greatest general in the world. Yah!" All this time I stood calm and fearless, knowing that at any moment the thousands of rifles levelled at my beautiful head might be discharged. Ever thoughtful of those weaker than myself, I placed Inki behind me, that the bullets might strike me first. Even the Boers were overcome with admiration at my undaunted bearing, and hesitated to fire.

5. Suddenly I remembered that we, knowing that the flag of truce might not protect us, had brought with us two large squirts filled with soap and water. At that moment Joubert gave the order to fire, and the whole commando let fly at us; but simultaneously I discharged the contents of my squirt full in Joubert's face. He leapt into the air with a fearful scream of agony. Although the Boers had never seen any soap and water, they had heard that the British executed Boer spies by washing them; and the appearance of this novel weapon filled them with terror. Volley after volley we poured into them, and finally the whole commando took flight, leaving thousands lying in terror and agony on the ground.

6. Do not, however, imagine that I had not suffered in this glorious engagement. On the contrary, I was literally riddled with bullets. Inki, who was standing behind me, and consequently escaped unhurt, assures me that he watched the whole fight through a hole in my chest, caused by a large shell. However, I am happy to say I am rapidly recovering. When, late that night, we marched into camp with 10,000 prisoners, we were greeted with such cheers as have probably never before been heard in South Africa. I noticed the traitor Yarnslinger hiding in his tent. I shall really have to chastise the low hound. I am the hero of the town, and every girl in the place is madly in love with your noble correspondent.

Big Budget 140; 17 February 1900 (Charles Genge)

THE LADYSMITH Nᵒ. OF THE Big Budget.

1ᵈ   1ᵈ

Vol. VI. No. 141.   WEEK ENDING SATURDAY, FEBRUARY 24, 1900.   Price One Penny.

Sir Redvers Buller, V.C., Commander-in-Chief of the Ladysmith Relief Force.

Sir Geo. White, V.C., Chief Commander of gallant Ladysmith, to whom this number is dedicated.

Sir Charles Warren, Commander of a Ladysmith Relief Force.

The brave garrison of Ladysmith watch the approach of their Comrades-in-Arms. Cheers ring out, and the guns are manned. Is relief at hand! It is a terribly anxious moment; but, stand or fall, Ladysmith has won the admiration of the world. May they have the good luck they deserve!

Big Budget 141; 24 February 1900

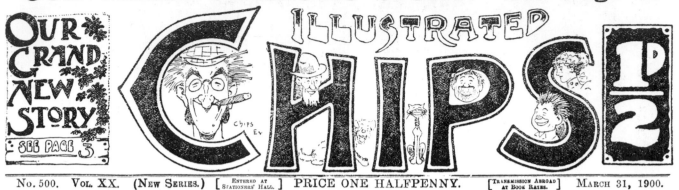

No. 500. VOL. XX. (NEW SERIES.) [ENTERED AT STATIONERS' HALL.] PRICE ONE HALFPENNY. [TRANSMISSION ABROAD AT BOOK RATES.] MARCH 31, 1900.

1. Poor Boers! Their luck was dead out; but worse was to come when Weary Willy and Tired Tim turned up at the front in their new motor-car. You see, they had come across to capture Kruger, and that's why Tim is got up as a Dutch maiden and Willy as a Boer cornet. "Good luck to you, old coughdrops!" shouted the Tommies, "and don't lose your fizwigs!" "Listen to that!" cooed Tim. "It must be my handsomeness that attracts them." "You—oh, yes!" snigged Willy; "you're as handsome as a tame faggot—my word!"

2. Still, pretty presently they got to the Boer camp just after old Kruger had finished his tea and winkles. "Ach! vot you call dis, mine leetle fat vrouw?" asked Uncle Paul, pointing to the motor. "Oh!" chimed in Tim, "that's something we found on the kopje—I mean sjambok—no—trek, veldt, rooinek, or blinkin' something—while the British Army was cutting off home. Goes all by its lone, without a single shove. You come and have a canter, Uncle." "Vell, I tinks I dakes a short stroll in dat," replied Kruger; "I vill get mineself inside."

3. "All aboard! Let her went! Pip-pip!" "Yow-oo-ooh! Vot der perliceman vos you doin'?" howled Uncle Paul. "You shdops dis ting immediatvonce, I toles you; an' I vos get oudt!" "Oh, yus, you nice, whiskery old gentleman," smiled Tim; "you'll get out presently—and suddint-like, too! Coo-ho!" "My opinion 'xactly!" piped Willy. "And tell that chap at the back to sit down, or he'll catch a draught in his coat-tails!"

4. How does this suit you, Uncle?" chuckled the pair, as the motor slid down the kopje. "Shakes yer orange free states up a bit, don't it?" "Oo-er! I vos tole you I don't like him," yelled Paul. "Vill you save dis old man, und I vos give you twopence?" "Go long, you silly little silly!" giggled Willy; "you ain't worth so much. You'll find that you'll be owing a bit when you come to settle up."

5. Sw-oo-sh! Kersplash! The car struck the river and shot straight across to the other side, where the Tommies were in waiting. "Ach! mine goot gootness!" yelled Uncle, "I vos a brisoner taken sometimes, aindt it?" "That's so, cocky!" chuckled Willy, "and they've got a few old scores to settle up with you—don't you fret. Now then, out you come—all of you!"

6. Then they stuck the old gent on a Neddy, and took him up to see the British generals. "'Twas me alone wot did this thing!" sang Tim. "Ditto repeato exactlio," piped Willy. "And if we don't get General Buller to stand a tripe supper on the strength of it—well, there'll be trouble for readers of CHIPS to look upon."

(Don't miss our next number—it will be a corker.)

DON'T MISS IT!

BRITAIN INVADED
OUR GREAT PATRIOTIC STORY.
See page 2.

ILLUSTRATED CHIPS 1d ½

No. 503. VOL. XX. (NEW SERIES.) [Entered at Stationers' Hall.] PRICE ONE HALFPENNY. [Transmission Abroad at Book Rates.] APRIL 21, 1900.

HOW PRETORIA WAS CAPTURED BY WEARY WILLY AND TIRED TIM!

1. Willy, Tim, and Gussie the Flea were on the trek. That means they were off again to worry the Boer chaps, and give CHIPS' readers a laugh. "Don't forget to bring old Kruger's whiskers back with you," roared the Tommies. "Not forgetting a cheer for the good old Margate Flea," piped Gussie from his little gun. "Toodleoo, chips!"

2. Then they came to the Modder (or some other river—it doesn't matter much), and in the middle a fearful yell was heard. "Ouch!" squeaked Willy, "I've taken a lump out o' me napper with this blinkin' whip! Somebody call up the hospital! Yow-ooh!" "Tut-tut! Don't be silly," smiled Tim. "I didn't feel it, so why all this fuss? Let's get along."

3. Now, our pals never take chances. So, when tea-time arrived, they fixed up their portable tin fort. "Pip-pip, Willy," sang Tim cheerily, "I saw you fust, up there. Peep bo!" "Gerrout, you barrel-chested crackpot!" piped Willy; "you're old enough to know better. Get on with the job, or I'll give you one on the boko with me coke-hammer!"

4. And directly the Union Jack went up the Boers spotted it, and came to make inquiries. "Give us a bunk up, uncle," said Van Hummingbug to Kruger. "I bet dot vos General Roberts and der British Army inside, anyways." "Oop!" panted Kruger, "we vos have 'em dis time, I bet my socks."

5. But those walls were made to fall down easily, and flatten out inquisitive people. "Vot the Bloemfontein are you up to?" howled Kruger. "You vos squeeze mine pertoka 'orribly! Yah-ooh!" "Good aftertea, uncle," smole Willy; "just wait a shake until we've finished our gargle, and then we'll attend to you."

6. "Now, gents, what's the row?" yelled our pals. "Please to remember there's real dum-dums in these shootin' irons fresh from the Boer laager." "Give me a chance," yelled Kruger; "let my pal have 'em—he vos do dot sort o' bizness. O-o-oh!" "Excuse me," whined Hummingbug, "but der goods vos useless to me—now I tole you."

7. "Then we'll have your whiskers!" smiled Willy and Tim. And have them they did! And leaving Gussie and the dog to guard the crowd, off they rode to Pretoria. "Say, Willy," mentioned Tim, "these old togs do buz a bit, don't they?" "Bear up, ole pal," chuckled Willy. "Hoo-roo for Tim Kruger the Second!"

8. And when they entered Pretoria the Boer crowd turned out to cheer, thinking that Kruger and Van Hummingbug had arrived. "Go it, my dusty brother bungling burghers," piped Tim, "we've snuffed the British Army, and collared Joe Chamberlain!" Whereupon the old gee got so excited that he kicked a Dutchman in the chin.

9. "Now, then," said Tim to the commandant, "hurry your men off to Bloemfontein, and give General Roberts a dot on his kitchener—and, mind you, if I catch any of you playing marbles on the road I'll bang yer across the snitch." "Yah! dot vos so," smiled the Dutchman. And off went the dusty crew. (And this isn't the finish. The rest of it is on page 8.)

Illustrated Chips 503; 21 April 1900

The comic peace was short-lived. Within the year, Willie and Tim were off to have a punch-up with the Boxers (p. 142). The century turned and was duly celebrated by *Big Budget* (p. 143), but seventeen days later the Queen was dead. The Edwardian era had begun: would it turn out as predicted (p. 144)?

10. And later on the pals opened the gates to let in the British Army. "Wotto! Bobs, me boy! come along in and make yourself at home," said Willy. "Much obliged, I'm sure," smiled our champion general; "and if you don't mind I'll ask all my boys in with me to take a muckle o' pinkle with you." "Why, certainly," chirped Tim. "Let 'em all come."

11. And wasn't it fun when the Boer Army, after finding they had been spoofed, returned, to find the British in possession! "What's the game?" asked Tommy Atkins, when Boer tried to climb the wall; "this is the Queen's private property." "Ach! is dot so?" howled the other Boers; "den der game vos oop, and ve trusts ole Kruger never no more."

12. Then the band played, and up went the British Flag with cheers. "Timmy, my noble friend," said Lord Roberts afterwards, "I appoint you Governor of Pretoria at thirty bob a week. And your old pal Willy is made Chief Officer of the canteen." (*But in next week's* CHIPS *you'll find them back home again playing up their monkey tricks as usual.*)

The Comic Artist
(index to artists)

Baxter, W. G.   2, 66
Browne, Tom   1, 3, 17, 28, 29, 30, 48, 53, 59, 61, 62, 82, 84, 85, 86, 87, 88, 89, 90, 93, 95, 96, 97, 100, 108, 110, 114, 117, 122, 123, 124, 125, 126, 135

Cavenagh, S. W.   50, 76
Chasemore, Archibald   5
Clarke, A. H.   46, 52, 75

Duval, Marie   26

'F.L.'   20
Fraser, George Gordon   57, 80, 81

Genge, Charles   37, 54, 109, 132, 133, 137
Gray, Alfred   42, 43, 56, 67, 94

Hill, Roland   18, 19, 21
Hodgson, Ralph   4, 22, 25, 31, 47, 83, 91, 92, 118, 127, 128, 129, 130, 131, 134, 136, 143
Holland, Frank   32, 38, 39, 49, 63, 70, 71, 72, 73

'Jan'   116

'M.A.B.'   74

O'Neill, H.   101

Thomas, W. Fletcher   27, 55, 78, 79, 102, 106, 120, endpapers

Veal, Oliver E.   19

Wilkinson, Ernest   24
Wilkinson, Frank   44, 60
Wilkinson, Tom   65, 77

Yeats, Jack Butler   40, 41, 45, 51, 58, 68, 69
'Yorick' (see Hodgson, Ralph)

ILLUSTRATED CHIPS

No. 518. Vol. XX. (New Series.) [Entered at Stationers' Hall.] PRICE ONE HALFPENNY. [Transmission Abroad at Book Rates.] August 4, 1900.

1. Wherever Weary Willy and Tired Tim appear there's bound to be trouble. The other afternoon, while old Professor Ricebags was sampling Southend winkles, the sweet innocents pinched his water-cycle, and did a skedoodle-doodle-do to see how things were going on in China. "Willy, me pigeon-chested pal, we're arrooved in the Celestial Land," piped Tim, "and in two shakes of a flapdaddle we'll be among the Boxers!" "Orlrite; don't sing it, cocky," sniggered Willy. "I'm a bit of a nib with the dukes meself. Back pedal, or you'll break something!"

2. Well, they got ashore all right, and were having a turn round in search of a muckle of pinkle when up stepped a mob of Boxers. "Oo-er," wailed Tim, "we never reckoned on having knives and forks with the china. What'll we do?" "Come on, you silly sossidge!" yelled Willy as he made a bee-line for the furthest point from the pigtails. "You know Auntie would be orful cross if she saw us talkin' to these bounders!" And the pair hooked it, with the Ching-changs on their heels yelling, "Chow-chow! Down wid the foreign debbils! Killee! killee! Yow!"

3. Now, as Willy and Tim had an appointment with the winkle man at the corner of Carmelite Street in three weeks' time, they didn't mean to be cotched. "Did you hear them, Willy?" breathed Tim. "They called us foreigners—sich impidence! I'm a good mind to hit one of 'em—strate, I am!" "Yes'm, I don't think," puffed Willy. "You come in here with me, or you'll find yourself served up as puppy pie!"

4. Luckily for Willy and Tim, they happened to drop inside the Purple Temple of the Cock-eyed Idol, and the Boxers didn't dare to follow in after them. But they waited Oh, yes, they did; and they weren't going to shift, neither, till the pals came out. But when two charming things with captivating dials popped out with a rush, the mob left in a hurry. "Pigtails and puppy soup!" growled the idols, "we'll have yer eyeballs if you don't shift!"

5. And in turn they mopped off on their water-cycle. "Junkpots and limejuice!" howled Tim as the sea-serpent bobbed up to pass the time of day, "'ere's our old pal the Yarmouth Bloater turned up again!" "Ease down," whimpered Willy; "I don't like the angry look of the fifth kink in his spine. Say something nice to him!" But the sea-serpent was right off. "Cods' roes and pickled cockles!" he snorted. "I am a bit peckish, certainly, but I'll bet a pound they're not fit to eat!"

6. So Willy and Tim floated gaily up to a British gunboat, and whistled on their fingers. "Cheer oh, admiral!" cried Tim; "we're more idol than idle this trip—d'ye twig?" "Don't I—rather!" yelled the other one. "Come aboard, and have a snifter, for we're jolly glad to see you again!" And did the pair go? Well, could they refuse anything on the cheap? But they couldn't stay long, for they had to hurry back to the Mile End Road to be in time for a thrilling adventure in next week's Chips.

Illustrated Chips 518; 4 August 1900

Vol. VIII. No. 186.   WEEK ENDING SATURDAY, JANUARY 5, 1901.   PRICE ONE PENNY.

ALF AND BILLY TRY TO CELEBRATE THE NEW CENTURY BY BEING VERY, VERY GOOD. WHAT HO!

1. "ALF," sighed Billy, "them there goody-goody-come-and-kiss-me kind of books says if yer good yer rappy. I've turned over a few leaves in me time at the noo year, but this is the fust bloomin' noo century I've ever struck. I mean ter go straight. Don't the worry thort make yer rappy?" And Alf said, "C-C-Course it d-d-does, chump 'ead. Carn't yer 'ear 'ow I'm larfin'?"

2. And, my gracious, didn't they start a treat! "Chuck 'em orl on," cackled Alf, "and we'll 'ave a howlin' bonfire. I ain't goin' ter smoke, or drink, or bet, or use norty words never again. Oh, don't I feel rappy!" "Me too," sighed Billy, "only I fink we'd better drink this fizz, 'cos it might put the fire out, and coals is dear." "Dump it hon" roared Alf.

3. Oh, it was a lovely couple of leaves that they turned over. That same night they strolled into the "Pork and Gridiron" and called for teetotal gargles. Who should be there but Bogey Bertie and 'Appy Ike, swigging beer. "Alf," sighed Billy, "jest look at them there depraved wretches. 'Ows yer lemmingade?" "Oh, grand," sobbed Billy. "It's—bootiful—so c-c-coolin'!"

4. Don't shudder, reader, please don't shudder. They actually were so good that they went to work! "Ain't it lovely, bein' good?" panted Alf, as he tried to bore a hole in a chunk of granite. "Don't it make yer rappy?" "Oh, be-yoo-tiful," moaned Billy. "I do love it, Alfy, only I wish I'd got me gloves, 'cos this 'ere job's raisir' blisters."

5. Then the next day came on its hind legs, and that stout gent floated past with the oof in his pocket. And when they'd got over the shock a bit Alf lisped, "Billy, we've been good for free days, ain't us?" "We 'ave! What ho!" "That bloke 'ad a red nose, 'adn't he, and 'e'll spend all that oof in drink. Let's rescue 'im!"

6. They did—at least, they rescued the notes out of his right-hand pocket. Two hours later Alf murmured, "Billy, old hoss, this is the rappiest moment of me life. It makes me swell wiv pride ter fink we've saved that fat cove from a drunkard's grave. Oh, we are good. Good 'ealth fer 1901, readers, and don't fergit us on the front page. We'll just hum, cockies."

Big Budget 186; 5 January 1901 (Ralph Hodgson)

143

1. IN the next century when all noises in the streets have to be done away with, we shall have noiseless German bands with muffled instruments.

2. And the costers will all have to be gagged.

3. Pa will read his **Big Budget** in peace then, 'cos all the kids will have to cry into the patent household noise tank.

4. Of course all the traffic will have to be silent. No wheels for the carts, and patent spring pads for horses' feet—not much noise then.

5. Polly will have to shut up, too.

6. Bobbies will carry the silent truncheon so that they won't make a noise when they hit you.

Big Budget 24; 27 November 1897